INFUSING REAL-LIFE TOPICS
INTO EXISTING CURRICULA

PRO-ED Series on Transition

Edited by
J. Patton
G. Blalock
C. Dowdy
T. E. C. Smith

INFUSING REAL-LIFE TOPICS INTO EXISTING CURRICULA

Recommended Procedures and Instructional Examples
for the Elementary, Middle, and High School Levels

James R. Patton
Mary E. Cronin
Susan J. Wood

8700 Shoal Creek Boulevard
Austin, Texas 78757-6897
800/847-3202 Fax 800/397-7633
Order online at http://www.proedinc.com

© 1999 by PRO-ED, Inc.
8700 Shoal Creek Boulevard
Austin, Texas 78757-6897
800/847-3202   Fax 800/347-7633
Order online at http://www.proedinc.com

Library of Congress Cataloging-in-Publication Data

Patton, James R.
    Infusing real-life topics into existing curricula : recommended
procedures and instructional examples for the elementary, middle,
and high school levels / James R. Patton, Mary E. Cronin, Susan J.
Wood.
        p.   cm. — (PRO-ED series on transition)
    Includes bibliographical references.
    ISBN 0-89079-814-1 (pbk : alkpaper)
    1. Handicapped children—United States—Life skills guides.
2. Handicapped children—Education—United States. 3. Handicapped
youth—United States—Life skills guides. 4. Handicapped youth—
Education—United States. 5. Life skills—Study and teaching—
United States. 6. Special education—United States—Curricula.
    I. Cronin, Mary E.   II. Wood, Susan J.   III. Title.   IV. Series.
HV888.5.P37   1999
371.9—DC21   99-13430
                                                                                CIP

This book is designed in New Century Schoolbook and Melior.

Production Director: Alan Grimes
Production Coordinator: Dolly Fisk Jackson
Managing Editor: Chris Olson
Art Director: Thomas Barkley
Designer: Jason Crosier
Print Buyer: Alicia Woods
Preproduction Coordinator: Chris Anne Worsham
Staff Copyeditor: Martin Wilson
Project Editor: Debra Berman
Publishing Assistant: John Means Cooper

Printed in the United States of America

1 2 3 4 5 6 7 8 9 10   03 02 01 00 99

This book is dedicated to those teachers and administrative staff who have helped shape and strengthen our thinking on the importance of teaching life skills to all students. Without their enduring support over the years, our voices would have long ago faded into the din of all the other voices proclaiming educational importance.

Contents

Preface to Series

The transition of students from school to adulthood roles has emerged as one of the most important topics in the field of special education and rehabilitation. The critical nature of planning for the transition needs of students has also been recognized in the school-to-work, often referred to as school-to-careers, initiative.

The PRO-ED Series on Transition evolved from a symposium convened in September 1994. Along with the opportunity for professionals interested in the practical aspects of the transition process to discuss many different issues, the symposium produced a series of papers that were published originally in the *Journal of Learning Disabilities* and subsequently in bound form as a book titled *Transition and Students with Learning Disabilities*. The current series represents an attempt to provide practical resources to transition personnel on a variety of topics that are critical to the process of preparing individuals for adulthood. Each book in the series contains valuable practical information on a specific transition topic. Titles in the series include:

- *Adult Agencies: Linkages for Adolescents in Transition*
- *Assessment for Transitions Planning*
- *Developing Transition Plans*
- *Family Involvement in Transition Planning and Implementation*
- *Follow-Up Studies: A Practitioner's Handbook*
- *Infusing Real-Life Topics into Existing Curricula: Recommended Procedures and Instructional Examples for the Elementary, Middle, and High School Levels*
- *Self-Determination Strategies*
- *Teaching Occupational Social Skills*
- *Transition from School to Young Adulthood: Basic Concepts and Recommended Practices*
- *Transition Issues Related to Students with Visual Disabilities*
- *Transition to Employment*
- *Using Community Transition Teams to Improve Transition Services*
- *Working with Students with Disabilities in Vocational–Technical Settings*

We hope that these resources will add to the growing body of materials designed to assist professionals involved in the transition process. The books in this series address the need for practical resources on transition that focus solely on specific topics.

Jim Patton, Ginger Blalock, Carol Dowdy, Tom Smith

Preface

This book expands upon concepts initially discussed in *Life Skills Instruction for All Students with Special Needs: A Practical Guide for Integrating Real-Life Content Into the Curriculum* (Cronin & Patton, 1993). In the 1993 book we presented a continuum for teaching life skills that included comprehensive life skill course development and infusing life skill information into existing course content. Our intent in writing the *Life Skills Instruction* book was to provide an array of instructional options for teachers to assist their students of varying abilities in acquiring skills for successful adult functioning. Since the publication of that book, many teachers, school administrators, and university faculty have encouraged us to expand the infusion option presented in the book because instructing all students in general education classes in the real-world application of content information has become a national goal through GOALS 2000: Educate America Act of 1994, the School-to-Work Opportunities Act of 1994, and the Secretary's Commission on Achieving Necessary Skills (SCANS) (1991) projects. This book is the result of that growing need.

In the compilation of this document, we were reaquainted with the complexities of obtaining copyright approval. We would like to acknowledge the following publishers who, by granting permissions to reprint pages from student textbooks, assisted us in making this book possible: Addison-Wesley Longman (Menlo Park, California); Glencoe McGraw Hill (Mission Hills, California); Holt, Rinehart and Winston (Orlando, Florida); Houghton Mifflin (Evanston, Illinois); PRO-ED, Inc. (Austin, Texas); Silver Burdett Ginn (Upper Saddle River, New Jersey); and Steck-Vaughn (Austin, Texas).

This book would not be in your hands had it not been for the generosity of others and the continued faith that sunny days do come eventually. We would like to recognize and acknowledge the professionals and their schools who were very generous in letting us search endlessly for just the right examples from student textbooks: Dr. Peggy Kirby and Jeanne Monte of the Jefferson Community School in Metairie, Louisiana; Dr. Roslyn Smith, Cynthia Horne, and Anita Williams of Areatha Castle Haley Elementary School in New Orleans, Louisiana; Barry Newberger and Gilly Jaunet of Jesuit High School, New Orleans, Louisiana; the teachers and administrators of Bishop Perry Middle School, New Orleans, Louisiana; Dr. Jay Miller and Sonja Yates, University of New Orleans; Robin Spencer, Austin, Texas; and all our students at the University of New Orleans and the University of Texas at Austin and their students who continue to remind us how important life skills are for all of us.

J. R. P., M. E. C., S. J. W.

CHAPTER 1
Teaching Real-Life Content

Preparing students with special needs for the transition from school to young adulthood is recognized as a comprehensive process that involves the development of knowledge and skills needed to meet the challenges of adulthood. The formal transition planning process, which occurs later in a student's school career, includes identifying needs, planning for them, and assuring that they are addressed. Although the implementation of a comprehensive transition process is valuable and mandated, it is nonetheless *reactive*. In other words, identifying transition needs at age 14 implies that educators are reacting to a student's transition needs profile.

A more desirable scenario is one that is *proactive* in terms of adult outcomes. In this conceptualization, a program of transition education, addressing various life demands associated with the different transition planning areas, is ongoing. It is described as proactive because, in such a system, transition education is not prescribed as a result of identified needs; it is provided as a natural and important part of the existing curriculum.

A number of ways exist for educators to cover real-life content. The major options are highlighted later in this chapter. The primary focus of this book, however, is on one of the ways to address the skills and knowledge needed in everyday life: infusing real-life content into existing curricula. This approach is emphasized for one very sound reason: It is the most likely approach to be used.

BASIC CONCEPTS

Background Information

The adult outcomes database for individuals with special needs paints a generalized picture of unemployment or underemployment, low pay, part-time work, frequent job changes, nonengagement with the community, limitations in independent functioning, and restricted social lives. The research that exists on adult outcomes, coupled with the data on dropout rates, is both illuminating and alarming and, as a result, continues to influence professional thinking, policy, and practice. Given that this less-than-favorable scenario has been evident for some years, and has not changed appreciably over time, tactics for better preparing students to deal with the many challenges of adulthood are urgently needed.

Based on what is known about adult outcomes for students with special needs and how they are prepared for postschool living, it is reasonable to conclude the following:

- Many individuals who spend time in special education are not being prepared for the multidimensional demands of adulthood.

- A significant percentage of the students who have special needs are not finding the school experience to be valuable, leading more than a few to drop out.

- The educational programs of many students in special education are not meeting current as well as future needs.

- Continuing (i.e., lifelong) educational opportunities for adults with special needs are warranted.

- Reexamination of the curricular structure of secondary special education programs is needed, and the availability of viable, alternative curricular options is desirable.

- Closer articulation across all levels of schooling (elementary to middle and middle to high school) is needed.

Definitions of Terms

The terms *real-life content* and *life skills* are used interchangeably in this book. Although many terms exist to refer to those skills needed to function successfully in adulthood (Cronin, 1996), these two phrases communicate the essence of what we are stressing in this book. Real-life content, or life skills, means specific competencies (i.e., knowledge and skills) of local and cultural relevance needed to perform everyday activities in a variety of settings typically encountered by most adults. As is highlighted in the definition, the nature of specific life skills can vary from one setting to another. For example, a number of life skills are involved in using any form of public transportation; however, the specific skills needed are very much a function of the city or locale where one lives.

RATIONALE FOR TEACHING LIFE SKILLS

Relationship of Life Skills to Adult Outcomes

The most convincing argument for the teaching of life skills is that the application of these competencies to some degree in various settings is essential for successful adult functioning. Having as many of these competencies as possible at one's disposal increases an individual's chances of working through the day-to-day challenges that come his or her way.

We discuss two models as examples of the adult domains that teachers should keep in mind when considering the goals of education for students with special needs. The two models chosen are the Domains of Adulthood model (Cronin & Patton, 1993) and the Life-Centered Career Education (LCCE) model (Brolin, 1997).

The overriding element of Cronin and Patton's (1993) model, adult domains, focuses on six areas of adult functioning:

- Employment/Education
- Home and Family
- Leisure Pursuits
- Community Involvement
- Physical/Emotional Health
- Personal Responsibility and Relationships

Adults need to have some degree of minimal competence and independence in each of these areas. These domains, along with 23 subdomains, serve as an arbitrary organizational framework from which one can consider the complexities of adulthood. Table 1.1 includes all of the subdomain areas.

TABLE 1.1

Models of Adult Functioning

Model	Adult Domain/ Curriculum Area	Subdomains/ Competency Areas
Domains of Adulthood (Cronin & Patton, 1993)	Employment/Education	General Job Skills General Education/Training Considerations Employment Setting Career Refinement and Re-evaluation
	Home and Family	Home Management Financial Management Family Life Child Rearing
	Leisure Pursuits	Indoor Activities Outdoor Activities Community/Neighborhood Activities Travel Entertainment
	Community Involvement	Citizenship Community Awareness Services/Resources
	Physical/Emotional Health	Physical Health Emotional Health
	Personal Responsibility and Relationships	Personal Confidence/Understanding Goal Setting Self-Improvement Relationships Personal Expression
Life Centered Career Education (Brolin, 1997)	Daily Living Skills	Managing Personal Finances Selecting & Managing a Household Caring for Personal Needs Raising Children & Meeting Marriage Responsibilities Buying, Preparing, & Consuming Food Buying & Caring for Clothing Exhibiting Responsible Citizenship Utilizing Recreational Facilities & Engaging in Leisure Getting Around the Community
	Personal-Social Skills	Achieving Self Awareness Acquiring Self Confidence Achieving Socially Responsible Behavior Maintaining Good Interpersonal Skills Achieving Independence Making Adequate Decisions Communicating with Others
	Occupational Guidance and Preparation	Knowing & Exploring Occupational Possibilities Selecting & Planning Occupational Choices Exhibiting Appropriate Work Habits & Behavior Seeking, Securing, & Maintaining Employment Exhibiting Sufficient Physical-Manual Skills Obtaining Specific Occupational Skills

Within the 23 subdomain areas, Cronin and Patton (1993) identified 147 major life demands that represent events typically encountered or required by adults in everyday life. A complete listing of these major life demands is provided in Appendix A. As might be expected, varying sets of specific life skills, as defined above, relate to each major life demand.

The other model that has been used in many school settings, Brolin's (1997) LCCE model; has the following major curriculum areas:

- Daily Living Skills
- Personal-Social Skills
- Occupational Guidance and Preparation

Under these three major curriculum areas are 22 competencies (see Table 1.1) and 97 subcompetencies (see Appendix B).

Articulation with the Transition Planning Process

The ultimate outcome of the transition planning process is to maximize the chances that an individual will deal successfully with the multifaceted demands of adulthood, thus leading to higher degrees of personal fulfillment. The immediate goal of this process is to provide as seamless a movement from school to young adulthood as possible by having a plan of action in place.

As emphasized previously, to function successfully in adulthood, one must have the knowledge and skills to handle the various situations that arise or to be able to access supports and services when needed. A student acquires these competencies or connects with the appropriate services through school-based, family-driven, or self-initiated activities. Although nobody is completely prepared for the realities of adulthood, some students are more ready for the "big show" than others. For many adolescents with special needs, significant gaps exist. Comprehensive transition planning, if conducted appropriately, attempts to even the playing field by providing a process to identify, plan for, and act on the needs students have in dealing with the complexities of life prior to the formal termination of schooling.

The areas typically addressed by life skills curriculum match closely with transition planning areas. Although no agreed-upon taxonomy of adult outcome domains exists, a sense of what is currently being considered as important adult domains can be gleaned from examining the transition planning areas of various states. The most common transition planning domains, as identified by Clark and Patton (1997), are the following (listed alphabetically):

- Community participation
- Daily living
- Employment
- Financial/income management
- Health
- Independent living (includes living arrangements)
- Leisure/recreation
- Postsecondary education
- Relationships/social skills
- Transportation/mobility
- Vocational training

The areas listed by Clark and Patton relate closely to the adult domains listed by Cronin and Patton (1993) and Brolin (1997), discussed in the previous section.

Therefore, life skills instruction is the logical means for educators to begin preparing students for adulthood. Comprehensive attention to life skills is likely to affect the transition planning process by minimizing the requirement to address an extensive set of transition needs later in the student's school career.

More Meaningful Instruction

Another reason that teachers may find teaching life skills appealing is that, by their very nature, life skills topics provide a way to make existing content more interesting, meaningful, and possibly relevant to students. Along with behavior management and instructional accommodation competencies, having a framework for adding variety to ongoing instruction via real-life content strengthens a special education teacher's repertoire.

It is important to distinguish between making content *meaningful* and making it *relevant*. Although these terms are used interchangeably in practice, they differ. Meaningful implies that a given topic has some degree of impact on one's life, perhaps in some future sense. Relevance, on the other hand, is not only meaningful but also timely in that it has impact on one's life now. It is typically easier to teach topics that are relevant to students. We consider all life skills topics to be meaningful, yet only some have immediate relevance. For example, a teacher could develop a powerful and meaningful lesson about retirement planning; however, its relevance is lost for many students because retirement is an issue they will not deal with until a much later time.

APPROACHES TO TEACHING LIFE SKILLS

The basic elements of life skills instruction should be included in the programs of all students with special needs. Clark, Field, Patton, Brolin, and Sitlington (1994) noted that such coverage should begin early in a student's school career and, without question, can be implemented in inclusive settings. The following discussion provides a framework upon which to conceptualize life skills instruction as a precursor to addressing the adult outcome needs of students.

Life Skills Models

Programs developed to prepare students with mild disabilities for adult roles in postschool situations have been noted in the literature for years. For example, Kolstoe and Frey's (1965) seminal efforts on work study programs clearly addressed the need for preparing students with mild retardation for community life. Although the underlying notion of readying students for life after school is not new, the amount of attention given to it has increased.

Some recent curriculum development efforts are noteworthy (see Table 1.2). Their similarities are numerous, as reflected in their materials, the content taught, and the types of suggested classroom activities. However, differences can typically be found, primarily in curriculum design. This variance is not surprising for, as Armstrong (1990) noted, every curriculum design establishes a somewhat different set of priorities and provides for a program developed to respond to a particular set of needs determined or considered important by any number of individuals (e.g., teachers, parents, students, researchers, curriculum developers, community leaders). The curricular models designed to prepare students for adult roles focus primarily on the introduction to and the acquisition of adult skills. Table 1.2, which

TABLE 1.2

Career Education and Life Skills Education Models

Source	Major Components
Life-Centered Career Education (LCCE) (Brolin, 1997)	Three major areas: • Daily living • Personal–social • Occupational guidance and preparation
Hawaii Transition Project (1987)	Four major areas: • Vocation education • Home and family • Recreation/leisure • Community/citizenship
Community-Referenced Curriculum (Smith & Schloss, 1988)	Five major areas: • Work • Leisure and play • Consumer • Education and rehabilitation • Transportation
Community Living Skills Taxonomy (Dever, 1988)	Five major areas: • Personal maintenance and development • Homemaking and community life • Vocational • Leisure • Travel
Life Problems of Adulthood (Knowles, 1990)	Six major areas: • Vocation and career • Home and family living • Enjoyment of leisure • Community living • Health • Personal development
Domains of Adulthood (Cronin & Patton, 1993)	Six major areas: • Employment/education • Home and family • Leisure pursuits • Community involvement • Physical/emotional health • Personal responsibility and relationships
Post-School Outcomes Model (National Center on Education Outcomes, 1993)	Seven major areas: • Presence and participation • Physical health • Responsibility and independence • Contribution and citizenship • Academic and functional literacy • Personal and social adjustment • Satisfaction

Note. Adapted from "Transition to Living: The Neglected Components of Transition Programming for Individuals with Learning Disabilities," by P. L. Sitlington, 1996. *Journal of Learning Disabilities, 29*, pp. 31–39, 52. Copyright 1996 by PRO-ED, Inc. Reprinted with permission.

is an adaptation of a more comprehensive one developed by Sitlington (1996), shows the major areas of focus of select models.

Programmatic Options

With a comprehensive list of major life demands or competencies available, it is possible to pursue the goal of teaching life skills. This can be accomplished either through the establishment of coursework that is life skills oriented or by integrating life skills topics into existing curricular content.

Coursework

One way to teach life skills is through a single course, titled Independent Living Skills or Skills for Life, that covers a variety of life skills. A more comprehensive approach is to create a series or set of life skills courses, with titles such as Personal Finance, Health and Hygiene, and Practical Communications. The titles and content of specific courses can vary according to situational needs. An example of a comprehensive course approach that was systematically implemented by the Dubuque, Iowa, Community Schools is described by Helmke, Havekost, Patton, and Polloway (1994).

Integration

Two techniques are available for integrating life skills topics into the existing curriculum: augmentation and infusion. The latter technique is the method on which this book is focused; however, augmentation also provides a viable means for covering real-life content.

With the *augmentation* method, the teacher dedicates a portion of the class period or part of the instructional week to specific life skills topics. This scheduling provides the opportunity to cover a particularly important life skills topic that is not typically covered in existing curricular scope and sequence.

The following example illustrates how augmentation can add important and relevant content to existing topics. Most consumer math texts cover the life skill of consumer credit options (i.e., associated with the major life demand of determining payment options for purchases). These commercial materials may not, however, cover essential techniques for paying with a credit card in specific situations. One such application is using a credit card at a self-serve gasoline pump. Textbooks neither capture the subtle differences in how different credit card gasoline pumps operate nor provide opportunities to use them. Yet, this type of information may be essential and relevant to some students.

The *infusion* approach capitalizes specifically on existing course content. The objective is to infuse into the material used in existing subject areas life skill topics that relate directly to information being covered. With this approach, close examination of course content is required to establish reference points on which life skills topics can be applied. This approach provides meaningfulness to course content taught on a daily basis. The attractiveness of the infusion approach is enhanced by the fact that infusion may be the only approach available when students are in inclusive settings, as a prescribed course of study is already in place.

Although we support the use of the infusion approach because it is relatively easy to use and therefore more likely to be implemented by teachers, it does come with one significant limitation. This approach does not guarantee comprehensive coverage of the range of topics that should be covered prior to the formal transition years, as the topics addressed are limited by the content encountered in the existing instructional materials. Nevertheless, this approach provides many opportunities to highlight important topics from which students can benefit.

PRACTICAL GUIDELINES FOR INFUSING LIFE SKILLS

As a conclusion to this chapter, we provide a list of guidelines that should be considered when using the infusion method of covering life skills.

1. Approach life skills instruction proactively rather than reactively.

2. Capitalize on as many opportunities to teach life skills that arise throughout the instructional day as is reasonable.

3. Be prepared for teachable moments.

4. Do not overwhelm yourself by thinking you have to cover everything or address all life skills opportunities.

5. Be sensitive to cultural and family values, interests, and preferences.

6. Generate a personal resource library or file of useful life skills related materials. Use the Internet for ideas and information.

7. Use whatever method is comfortable to you for integrating life skills content into existing curricula.

8. Enhance classroom-based instruction with community-based opportunities.

9. Attempt to make life skills being covered relevant as well as meaningful to students.

10. Recognize that infusing life skills content into existing curricula of general education not only is valuable to students with special needs who are in these settings but also benefits other students in inclusive settings by making lessons more interesting and real-life oriented.

CHAPTER 2

Recommended Procedures for Infusing Life Skills Content

The infusion approach to covering life skills is attractive because it does not require extensive amounts of time and energy from teachers. It works best when the teacher is aware of a set of procedures for capitalizing on opportunities to address important adult-referenced topics. The primary purpose of this chapter is to provide an organizational framework that is easily implemented within the ongoing instructional process. A secondary purpose for the chapter, which has a practical bent as well, is the identification of select resources that have been found to be extremely useful for providing information related to life skills.

The operative word associated with the infusion method is *opportunity*. It is very important that teachers take advantage of as many opportunities as possible to touch on topics that have life skills implications. The amount of time dedicated to real-life topics that arise from existing content may range from momentary to a significant amount of time. Ultimately, a balance must be achieved between the essentials of the explicit curriculum (the formal and stated curriculum) and the hidden curriculum (the actual curriculum implemented in the classroom, which would include life skills infusion coverage). A more detailed explanation of curriculum types is provided by Hoover and Patton (1997).

An example in which a teacher committed a significant amount of class time to take advantage of an opportunity to talk about real-life issues was described by Rossman (1983) in his article "The Cheese: An Essay on Method in Science Teaching." Rossman's narrative of capitalizing on a teachable moment clearly shows how one can integrate life skills topics into a science class:

> As I settle in with the fourth-graders on the rug, amid the usual horseplay, someone says it: "Who cut the cheese?" Much nose-pinching, a convulsion of giggles.
>
> I realize I've been given my lesson for the day. To avoid distraction, I tuck discreetly behind me the fossils I had brought as I ask, "Why do we call it 'cut the cheese'?"
>
> "It's like Limburger," they tell me. Most know that name, though it turns out that only two have actually tasted or smelled it.
>
> "So what do we call it besides 'cut the cheese'?"
>
> Someone says "pass wind," another volunteers "farting." More giggles, but only a few. They have grown so accustomed to frank discussion of frank terms for biological functions that the shock value is almost gone, and they refocus their attention quickly, in anticipation of the now-familiar routine of domesticating a highly charged subject.
>
> "Does anyone know the fancy name for farting, the formal name?" I ask. They have welcomed the idea of two vocabularies and pronounce *feces* and *saliva* like veterans now—though they don't quite grasp *why* one should be spared embarrassment in adult company by using Latinate words.

One of the typical comments shared by teachers after having read or listened to an account of Rossman's science lesson is that few teachers might be as knowledgeable as Rossman was, especially on the spot, of the biology of flatulence. Without question, he was able to pull off this spontaneous lesson that included a wealth of real-life issues better than most teachers would be able to do. As a matter of fact, few teachers would be able to go into the depth he did without a substantial amount of preparation and study about digestion. This example has to be understood as one in which a talented teacher was at work. Nevertheless, most teachers, with the right tools, are capable of making the mandated curriculum more real-life relevant in ways that are engaging to students.

With certain preparatory activities, most teachers can be ready to infuse creative teaching into the ongoing routine and existing content of the courses they are instructing. Some will be able to do so with amazing spontaneity; most will benefit from some preparation. The next section of this chapter presents a procedure for being prepared.

STEP-BY-STEP PROCEDURE

The infusion technique is composed of a basic four-step procedure:

1. Familiarity with the comprehensive set of knowledge and skills needed in adulthood (i.e., life skills)

2. Identification of places in the existing curriculum that can be associated with real-life topics

3. Planning life skills infusion activities

4. Actual instruction of life skills during ongoing lessons

There is nothing magical about the sequence of activities described; however, the main elements of each step are critical for successfully infusing real-life content into the curriculum.

1. Familiarity with the Demands of Adulthood

It is extremely helpful to have some frame of reference for conceptualizing the array of demands with which adults must deal on a daily basis. The models discussed in the previous chapter—see Tables 1.1 and 1.2—can be used for this purpose. All of the life skills education models highlighted in Table 1.2 provide schemata for understanding the everyday needs of adults. Two in particular, the Life-Centered Career Education model (Brolin, 1995) and the Domains of Adulthood model (Cronin & Patton, 1993), feature a comprehensive perspective of adult outcomes that is easy for teachers to conceptualize and utilize.

As for most frequently executed activities, the need to refer to a model, such as either of the two suggested above, will decrease with experience. Teachers likely will not need to be reminded of the major competencies or life demands once they begin to infuse life skills topics on a regular basis. However, teachers may want to refer to these models for guidance from time to time. With this in mind, teachers might want to copy Table 1.1 and have it readily available as they use the infusion technique.

2. Identification of Places in the Existing Curriculum that Can Be Associated with Real-Life Topics

It should go without saying that teachers need to be very familiar with the content that they are going to cover in their lessons along with the content that they assign students to read. With the infusion approach, teachers need to be vigilant for those opportunities to connect to real-life topics any content that arises during the course of their lessons or in the curricular materials being used by students.

We recommend that teachers thoroughly examine the instructional materials that students use and note where an "infusion moment" can occur. We recommend noting these moments either on an infusion form or in instructors' manuals that accompany the student materials.

In the beginning stages of attempting the infusion technique, teachers may find it helpful to use a planning guide to help organize this task. Two examples of such guides can be found in Appendix C. (These may be copied for use.) Like formalized lesson plan formats that are introduced in teacher training, a life skills infusion guide can be modified according to a teacher's particular needs. Nevertheless, a guide has instructional usefulness for demonstrating how to infuse life skills topics.

Alternatively, teachers can identify infusion reference points in their instructors' manuals, either by marking directly in the manual or using tags. Ideally notes could be written on the student book pages, which are typically reproduced in the teacher's manual.

Although such planning does require time and effort, it is not as demanding as it may seem at first. We feel that looking for opportunities to infuse life skills topics often is exciting for teachers because the activities that can be implemented as a result of infusion add variety to the instructional regimen. Moreover, as noted, the more frequently one undertakes this infusion planning, the easier it becomes.

Two positive student outcomes emerge from using this approach: (1) students are exposed to topics that can be beneficial to them immediately or at some point in the not-too-distant future, and (2) they become more engaged in ongoing instruction. For many teachers, the ultimate validation for infusing life skills topics into the curriculum will be the latter point—the positive reaction of students to this instructional tactic.

Although the next chapter provides numerous infusion examples taken from textbooks across all levels of schooling, it is useful to explain the process at this time. Figure 2.1 shows six pages from Level 6 of the Reading Milestones program. These pages demonstrate that many readings can be used as a springboard for infusing life skills topics. In the example depicted in Figure 2.1, both textual material and graphics are used as a way of relating this material to real-life contexts.

Before we explain the process further, a preliminary note is essential. Although many life skills topics could be infused into a reading series, we are not suggesting that all of these opportunities should be utilized. Rarely would a teacher be able to take advantage of all potential opportunities, particularly given the limitations of time. However, as one gets more facile in identifying infusion reference points, one is likely to become more masterful at covering a significant number of life skills topics.

Due to time constraints, teachers may want to capitalize on those opportunities that can be handled in what we call "infusion bursts." Much like the concept of lecture bursts (E.A. Polloway, personal communication, 1986), this tactic features quick coverage of a topic so as not to disrupt the flow of ongoing instruction

2

My Mom, the Mechanic

(continues)

FIGURE 2.1. Sample reading. From *Reading Milestones: An Alternative Reading Program*, Level 6, Orange Reader 9 (2nd ed., pp. 1, 3–5, 7–8), by S. P. Quigley, C. M. King, P. L. McAnally, and S. Rose, 1991, Austin, TX: PRO-ED. Copyright 1991 by PRO-ED, Inc. Reprinted with permission.

3

Kevin was doing his homework at the kitchen table when Mom walked into the room. Kevin thought she looked very funny.

"I like your new clothes," he called. Kevin tried hard not to laugh at her.

His mom was wearing a pair of Dad's old coveralls. Dad used the coveralls to keep his clothes clean when he worked on cars. The coveralls were too big for Mom, and, of course, she had had to roll up the sleeves and pant legs. Mom had a scarf on her hair, too.

(continues)

FIGURE 2.1. *Continued.*

4

"Well, I'm ready," Mom said to Dad.

Dad chuckled and led the way to the garage. "Let's go!"

Dad was the owner of a service station. He was a good mechanic, and he had a good business.

Now, Mom had gotten it into her head that she wanted to learn about cars, too. Kevin's mom always wanted to learn about new things. But, Kevin couldn't understand, "Why did she want to learn about cars?"

Dad didn't understand Mom's reasons either, but he was willing to teach her.

Mom thought that it would be good for her to know about cars. "I need to know in case of an emergency in the future," she said.

Kevin guessed that Dad agreed with her. He chuckled again as he watched his parents.

(continues)

FIGURE 2.1. *Continued.*

5

Kevin heard his dad open the hood of the car. "Today I will teach you about doing a simple tune-up," Dad said. "We will change the oil and the oil filter. You should change the oil and oil filter every 3,000 miles. When you have driven another 3,000 miles after today, we will need to change them again. Changing the oil and oil filter helps to keep the engine clean."

(continues)

FIGURE 2.1. *Continued.*

7

All afternoon, Kevin listened to his parents as they worked in the garage. Sometimes they worked quietly, and sometimes they worked noisily. He could hear Dad give directions and Mom reply.

Finally Kevin heard his parents coming in from the garage. They were laughing and talking.

"Well, I did it! I did a tune-up on the car," Mom said happily to Kevin. "It was hard work, but I did it, didn't I?"

"Yes, you did," Dad agreed. "I'm proud of you. You did a good job."

(continues)

FIGURE 2.1. *Continued.*

8

Kevin looked at his mom and laughed. It was a good thing that she was wearing Dad's coveralls because there was grease all over her clothes. She had grease on her nose, cheeks, and arms too.

Kevin shook his head and proudly said, "Look at her. That's my mom, the mechanic."

FIGURE 2.1. *Continued.*

of the main topic at hand. In this fashion, the teacher would bring up the life skills topic, act on it in whatever way is deemed appropriate (discussion of a question, quick generation of a list, etc.), and move on. All of this would occur in a rather rapid sequence of events.

On the other hand, often determined by the importance or timeliness of a life skill, a significant amount of time might be dedicated to the life skills topic. In this scenario, the ongoing lesson would be interrupted for a longer period of time, as Rossman (1983) did. Typically, such an interruption does not impair the integrity of the planned lesson.

At this point, we will demonstrate the use of the two planning approaches mentioned previously. The first sample utilizes the Life Skills Infusion Planning Guide (see Appendix C), and the second utilizes the more abbreviated planning process involving the use of the teacher's manual.

The story shown in Figure 2.1, "My Mom, the Mechanic," provides some nice opportunities for infusing life skills topics. Some possible ideas are presented in the completed Planning Guide (see Figure 2.2). Even nontextual material, such as the drawing on the first page of the story, can be the catalyst for covering certain issues (in this case, gender stereotyping), as indicated in Figure 2.2.

Use of the teacher's manual provides an alternative to the use of a predesigned form. This method is likely to be more appropriate for teachers who are comfortable with the infusion approach and do not need much prompting to launch into a discussion of real-life content. An example of this practice, using the story introduced above, is demonstrated in Figure 2.3.

3. Planning Life Skills Infusion Activities

Once the reference points for a set of infusion moments have been identified, some planning as to how to address them is required. Given, for the most part, that a significant amount of time is not available for each infusion topic, the teacher might be limited to certain types of activities.

The most likely choice of activities that can reasonably be implemented with the infusion approach include a quick question requiring brief responses; listing of information; description of a sequence of tasks that need to be performed; and personal examples. In "My Mom, the Mechanic," the "tools" reference point (as indicated in Figure 2.3) could elicit responses from students about tools that can be found at home; or it could prompt the teacher to have students generate a list of basic tools one might want to have at home. Figure 2.2 includes many other ideas and activities for this story.

4. Actual Instruction of Life Skills During Ongoing Lessons

The last step in the infusion process is straightforward. After the infusion points have been identified and instructional ideas have been considered, all that remains is the actual instructional phase. A teacher might want to identify these infusion moments with some type of spoken tagline that students will recognize. Two examples of such prompts are "It's time for a real world check" and "It's time for a life skills link." We also recommend that teachers provide a brief overview of what they plan to do during infusion moments.

Teachers should get into the habit of evaluating their infusion activities. Keeping notes on how well an infusion moment went along with some comments on what might work better next time is highly recommended.

Life Skills Infusion Planning Guide

Note: This planning guide is recommended for use when identifying content in existing curricular materials that can be linked to life skills topics.

Subject Area _____Reading_____   **Material** _Reading Milestones, Level 6, Book 9_

Content Referent	Possible Life Skills Topics	Notes
		[adult domains]
Picture of mom (p. 2)	• Discuss woman as a mechanic.	• Employment/Education
	• List tools needed around home— Where is a good place to buy tools?	• Home and Family
"Coveralls" (p. 3)	• Name occupations that require special clothes or uniforms.	• Employment/Education
"Learn about cars" (p. 4)	• Ask: Where could one learn more about cars?	• Community Involvement
	• Ask: Why is it a good idea to know your car works?	• Home and Family
	• Point out that some people do this as a hobby—Ask: What are some other hobbies parents have?	• Leisure Pursuits
"Change the oil" (p. 5)	• Discuss options for getting oil changed.	• Community Involvement
	• Discuss costs involved.	• Home and Family
"Worked noisily" (p. 7)	• List potential problems of a noisy workplace.	• Physical/Emotional Health
	• Ask: How can one reduce noise levels?	• Employment/Education
"Well, I did it" (p. 7)	• Ask: How did mom feel after finishing the tune-up?	• Personal Responsibility and Relationships
"Grease" (p. 8)	• Ask: How can one clean clothes?	• Home and Family
	• Ask: What is good to do after working in settings like a garage?	• Physical/Emotional Health

FIGURE 2.2. Life Skills Infusion Planning Guide, completed for use with "My Mom, the Mechanic" (Figure 1.1).

(continues)

FIGURE 2.3. Use of teacher's manual for infusion approach to using "My Mom, The Mechanic." From *Reading Milestones: An Alternative Reading Program*, Level 6, Orange Reader 9 (2nd ed., pp. 1, 3–5, 7–8), by S. P. Quigley, C. M. King, P. L. McAnally, and S. Rose, 1991, Austin, TX: PRO-ED. Copyright 1991 by PRO-ED, Inc. Reprinted with permission.

Kevin was doing his homework at the kitchen table when Mom walked into the room. Kevin thought she looked very funny.

"I like your new clothes," he called. Kevin tried hard not to laugh at her.

uniform — His mom was wearing a pair of Dad's old (coveralls.) Dad used the coveralls to keep his clothes clean when he worked on cars. The coveralls were too big for Mom, and, of course, she had had to roll up the sleeves and pant legs. Mom had a scarf on her hair, too.

FIGURE 2.3. *Continued.*

USEFUL RESOURCES

In addition to the life skills resources discussed earlier in this chapter, other materials can be very helpful in teaching practical, functional real-life topics. Certain types of reference books have come in handy in our infusion efforts. All teachers need to consult sources about some topics. A short list of useful books is provided in Table 2.1.

The Internet is a wonderful vehicle for finding information on almost any topic imaginable. It is helpful to be familiar with the different search engines and how they operate. World Wide Web sites useful for teaching life skills can be located in Web yellow pages books available in most bookstores. Table 2.2 provides a sampling of such Web sites.

TABLE 2.1

A Life Skills Resource List

Blumenthal, L. A. (1977). *The art of letter writing: The new guide to writing more effective letters for all occasions.* New York: Pedigree Books.

Boardroom Classics. (1991). *The book of inside information.* New York: Author.

Bragonier, R., & Fisher, D. (1990). *What's what: A visual glossary of the physical world* (Rev. ed.). Maplewood, NJ: Hammond.

Carrell, A. (1990). *Best home hints from the super handyman.* Dallas: Taylor Publishing.

Eisenberg, R., & Kelly, K. (1986). *Organize yourself.* New York: Macmillan.

Farmer's Almanac. (1993). *The old farmer's almanac: 1994.* Dublin, NH: Author.

Heloise. (1974). *Hints from Heloise: Over 2,000 easy, inexpensive, ingenious, and time-saving tips.* New York: Avon.

Jackson, A., & Day, D. (1979). *Tools and how to use them.* New York: Knopf.

Macauley, D. (1988). *The way things work: From levers to lasers, cars to computers—A visual guide to the world of machines.* New York: Houghton Mifflin.

Maggio, R. (1990). *How to say it: Choice words, phrases, sentences, and paragraphs for every situation.* Englewood Cliffs, NJ: Prentice-Hall.

Makower, J. (Ed.). (1986). *The map catalog: Every kind of map and chart on Earth and even some above it.* New York: Tillden Press.

Mary Ellen. (1979). *Mary Ellen's best hints: Fast-easy-fun ways of solving household problems.* New York: Warner Books.

McLoone-Basta, M., & Siegel, A. (1985). *The kid's world almanac of records and facts.* New York: World Almanac Publications.

New York Public Library. (n.d.). *Most frequently asked questions.* New York: Author.

Philbin, T., & Ettlinger, S. (1988). *The complete illustrated guide to everything sold in hardware stores.* New York: Macmillan.

Reader's Digest. (1977). *Fix-it yourself manual.* Pleasantville, NY: Author.

Reader's Digest. (1986). *How to do just about anything.* Pleasantville, NY: Author.

Schlesinger, A. M. (1993). *The world almanac and book of facts: 1994.* Mahawah, NJ: World Alamanac.

Schmitt, R. D. (1987). *Your child's health: A pediatric guide for parents.* New York: Bantam Books.

Ubell, V., & Sumberg, D. (1982). *Checklists: 88 essential lists to help you organize your life.* New York: Crown Publishers.

Willson, S. (Ed.). (1991). *Popular mechanics home answer book.* New York: Hearst Books.

TABLE 2.2

World Wide Web Sources

The following list of World Wide Web addresses provides a sampling of Web sites that can be used to locate life skills instructional resources

Consumer Reports
www.ConsumerReports.org

Kodak Guide to Better Pictures
www.kodak.com/global/en/consumer/picturetaking

American Library Association Parents Page
www.ala.org/parentspage

Internal Revenue Service
www.irs.ustreas.gov

Animal Network
www.petchannel.com

AMA Health Insight
www.ama-assn.org/consumer.htm

Best Fares Online
www.bestfares.com

Britannica Online
www.eb.com

The Weather Channel
www.weather.com

Home Improvement
www.nari.org

Holiday Celebrations
www.holidays.net

Job Locator
www.jobdirect.com

CNN
www.cnn.com

Get Healthy
www.healthfinder.gov

CHAPTER 3

Instructional Examples for Infusing Life Skills Topics into the Curriculum

This chapter provides 17 examples of the infusion technique discussed in the previous chapter. Seven of the examples are at the elementary level, five at the middle school level, and five at the high school level. Within each level, samples from several of the course content areas (reading, literature, mathematics, science, and social studies) are given. Each example includes a page from a student textbook and an accompanying infusion planning guide. The infusion planning guide helps organize and document the life skills topics presented in each class, subject, chapter, or unit, as highlighted in Chapter 2.

The purpose of these examples is to show several different ways the infusion approach can work at all levels and in different content classes. Three to six words (*reference points*) have been chosen from each student textbook page. At least one suggested life skill topic is given per word; however, many life skill topics could be generated for certain words. The choice of which life skill topic(s) to select for a 2- to 4-minute infusion moment will depend on the current needs of the students in the class and the available class time. Many classes may have time for only one life skill topic to be embellished, whereas other classes might be able to accommodate embellishment of three or four life skill topics. Whatever life skill topics are chosen, they should be relevant to the particular group of students.

Four practice infusion exercises, representing different school levels and content areas, can be found in Appendix D. These exercises include sample student textbook pages and blank Life Skills Infusion Planning Guides. The blank Planning Guide that accompanies each passage is the same as that presented in Chapter 2. The "Notes" column can be used for any number of purposes, such as indicating the adult domain that relates to the life skills topic being covered. Other purposes, such as specifying materials one might want to use in addressing the life skills topic, could also be listed in this column. (Blank planning forms for duplication can be found in Appendix C.)

ELEMENTARY LEVEL EXAMPLES

Name _____

Problem Solving
Using Data From a Chart

Use your coin punchouts.
Get coins for each amount in
the problem. Count to find
the total amount. Then write
the answer.

Junior Zoo Keeper Pay Chart	
Job	Pay
Feeding fish	25¢
Sweeping the sidewalk	30¢
Cleaning fish tanks	35¢
Selling bird food	20¢
Picking up litter	45¢
Selling zoo books	40¢

1. Raúl fed the fish and
   cleaned the fish tanks.
   What was his total pay?

   His total pay was ____ .

2. Ginger swept the sidewalk
   and picked up litter. How much
   money did she earn?

   She earned ____ .

3. Bing sold bird food one day.
   He sold zoo books the next day.
   How much did he earn in all?

   He earned ____ in all.

4. Andrea did three jobs. She sold
   bird food, swept the sidewalk,
   and cleaned the fish tanks.
   What was her total pay?

   Her total pay was ____ .

Content Referent	Possible Life Skills Topics	Adult Domain
Zoo	• Name the types of jobs found at the zoo.	Employment/Education
Fish	• List the types of supplies you would need for a fish.	Home and Family
Litter	• How can you help your community remain litter free? • Participate in a community cleanup or organize one around the perimeter of the school.	Community Involvement
Job	• How does completing a job make you feel?	Physical/Emotional Health
Litter	• How can litter affect your life? • What happens to litter? • What is your responsibility when you see litter?	Personal Responsibility and Relationships

Subject Area:	Math
Type of Material:	Textbook
Grade Level:	2nd grade
Book Title/Page:	*Addison-Wesley Mathematics*, page 201
Authors:	R. Eicholz, P. O'Daffer, R. Charles, S. Young, C. Barnett, C. Fleenor, S. Clemens, C. Thornton, A. Reeves, and J. Westley
Publisher:	Addison-Wesley Longman
Copyright Date:	1991

The girls   get   on the bus.
The boys   get   on the bus.
The man   gets   on the bus.

From *Reading Milestones: An Alternative Reading Program*, Level 2, Blue Reader 10 (2nd ed., p. 73), by S. P. Quigley, C. M. King, P. L. McAnally, and S. Rose, 1991, Austin, TX: PRO-ED. Copyright 1991 by PRO-ED, Inc. Reprinted with permission.

Content Referent	Possible Life Skills Topics	Adult Domain
Bus	• Identify the types of buses in your community. • Name the closest school bus stop to school and to your home.	Community Involvement
Bus	• List safety steps you should follow when you get off the bus.	Physical/Emotional Health
Bus	• Describe how you should behave on a bus. • Give two reasons why it is important to behave appropriately on a bus.	Personal Responsibility and Relationships

Subject Area:	Reading
Type of Material:	Reading Book Series
Grade Level:	2nd Grade
Book Title/Page:	*Reading Milestones*, Level 2, Blue Book 10 (2nd ed.), page 73
Authors:	S. P. Quigley, C. M. King, P. L. McAnally, and S. Rose
Publisher:	PRO-ED
Copyright Date:	1991

From *Reading Milestones: An Alternative Reading Program*, Level 3, Yellow Reader 6 (2nd ed., p. 19), by S. P. Quigley, C. M. King, P. L. McAnally, and S. Rose, 1991, Austin, TX: PRO-ED. Copyright 1991 by PRO-ED, Inc. Reprinted with permission.

Content Referent	Possible Life Skills Topics	Adult Domain
Tools	• Name various occupations and identify what tools each occupation may use (e.g., plumber–wrench, engineer–calculator, teacher–chalk).	Employment/Education
Tools	• Identify some tools you see your mom and dad use around the house.	Home and Family
Tools	• Name two places where you can buy tools.	Community Involvement
Help	• Describe what you would do if you saw someone who needed help.	Personal Responsibility and Relationships

Subject Area:	Reading
Type of Material:	Reading Book Series
Grade Level:	3rd grade
Book Title/Page:	*Reading Milestones*, Level 3, Yellow Book 6 (2nd ed.), page 19
Authors:	S. P. Quigley, C. M. King, P. L. McAnally, and S. Rose
Publisher:	PRO-ED
Copyright Date:	1991

Estimating Decimal Sums and Differences

Trail Map

LEARN ABOUT IT

EXPLORE Study the Map

Megan is planning a backpacking trip. She does not want to hike more than 15 km a day. Can she hike from the Ranger Station to Eagle Rock Ridge in one day?

TALK ABOUT IT

1. Is the distance from the Ranger Station to the Boat Dock closer to 3 or 4 kilometers? Explain.

2. To estimate the distance from the Ranger Station to Bear Mountain Pass, you could add front-end digits and get 3 + 4, or 7 km. Is this an overestimate or an underestimate?

You can round decimals when you want to estimate a sum to decide if it is close to a reference point.

3.7 km + 4.8 km + 2.3 km = ‖‖

■ round down, using front-end digits   3 + 4 + 2 = 9

■ round up   4 + 5 + 3 = 12

■ round to a chosen place   4 + 5 + 2 = 11

The estimates are under 15 km.

rounded to the nearest whole number

TRY IT OUT

Estimate these sums or differences by rounding as indicated. Tell whether the answer is an *overestimate* or an *underestimate*.

1. 5.8 + 6.7 (up)   **2.** 17.4 − 6.5 (down)   **3.** 9.56 + 8.78 (up)

Content Referent	Possible Life Skills Topics	Adult Domain
Ranger station	• Identify jobs related to the environment other than park ranger.	Employment/Education
Hike	• Name the places you and your family like to hike.	Home and Family
Backpacking	• List items you would need for a day-long backpacking trip.	Leisure Pursuits
	• List items you would need for an overnight trip.	
Backpacking	• Identify different organizations that regularly go backpacking (e.g., Boy/Girl Scouts, hiking clubs).	Community Involvement
Boat dock	• List some safety tips to remember when you go boating.	Physical/Emotional Health
Hike	• List ways in which you can be a responsible camper.	Personal Responsibility and Relationships

Subject Area:	Math
Type of Material:	Textbook
Grade Level:	4th grade
Book Title/Page:	*Addison-Wesley Mathematics,* page 424
Authors:	R. Eicholz, P. O'Daffer, R. Charles, S. Young, C. Barnett, C. Fleenor, S. Clemens, C. Thornton, A. Reeves, and J. Westley
Publisher:	Addison-Wesley Longman
Copyright Date:	1991

The children did not like to hear arguing. The boys asked Jenny, "What is wrong? Why are Mom and Dad fighting?"

Jenny could not answer the question. She hugged Ian and Bruce. Then Mom and Dad came into the room. They looked very unhappy. Bruce, Ian, and Jenny did not laugh. They all felt very sad, and they were scared. Everyone in the family was worried.

Content Referent	Possible Life Skills Topics	Adult Domain
Fighting	• List some people whose job it is to resolve differences that people have.	Employment/Education
Family	• List some of your family rules.	Home and Family
Family	• List some of the fun activities that you and your family do.	Leisure Pursuits
Fighting	• Describe how you feel when you have been in a fight.	Physical/Emotional Health
	• Describe how it makes you feel when two people in your family argue.	

Subject Area:	Reading
Type of Material:	Reading Book Series
Grade Level:	5th grade
Book Title/Page:	*Reading Milestones*, Level 5, Brown Book 1 (2nd ed.) (2nd ed.), page 22
Authors:	S. P. Quigley, C. M. King, P. L. McAnally, and S. Rose
Publisher:	PRO-ED
Copyright Date:	1991

LESSON **1**

A Changing America

THINK ABOUT WHAT YOU KNOW
What are some advantages of living in cities? What are some disadvantages?

STUDY THE VOCABULARY
baby boom   skyscraper

FOCUS YOUR READING
How did American life change in the years just after World War II?

A. The Nation's Population Is Young

The Baby Boom Every hundred years in this study of our country's history, we have paused to take a look at America. We have now reached 1950, and it is time to look at an imaginary "photograph" of America, just as we did for the year 1850. In 1950 your grandparents were probably young adults. In this portrait of our country, you will see that much about their lives is familiar to you. But you will also see ways in which life in 1950 was different from your life today.

The first thing to notice about the America of 1950 is the great number of young children. The Second World War had ended just five years before. You'll recall from Chapter 23 that the war had disrupted life for almost every American. One big change was that young people put off getting married. After the war, Americans were eager to get back to normal living. With renewed hope for the future, millions of young men and women were married and started families. These young families had so many children that the years from the mid-1940s through the 1950s became known as the baby boom.

An Economic Boom The baby boom affected the United States in many ways. Almost immediately it helped bring an economic boom, as new houses and other buildings were built for the new families. Young parents needed such goods as food, clothing, and even toys for their children. As children of the baby boom grew older, companies began to make products to sell to young buyers themselves — bikes, records, and fashions. And communities had to build more schools and hire more teachers for the swelling numbers of students.

B. Cities Grow in All Parts of the Nation

Population Shifts By 1950 more than two of every three Americans lived in or near a city. Cities had grown into immense places. There were five cities with over 1 million people. You'll remember that no city in the nation had even close to a million people in 1850. You can read more about American cities on page 564.

And by 1950 big cities were found in every part of the country. The fastest-growing cities were in the South and the Southwest. As you learned earlier, this area is known as the Sunbelt because the climate is mostly warm and sunny. The big move to the Sunbelt started during World War II. People moved there to take jobs in aircraft factories and in shipyards.

After the war many of the newcomers stayed on. The climate and job opportunities attracted still others to the Sunbelt. By 1950, millions were moving to this area and increasing the size of its cities. The city of Houston, Texas, for example, doubled in population in just ten years. Other cities like San Diego, California, and Baton Rouge, Louisiana, also grew rapidly.

Content Referent	Possible Life Skills Topics	Adult Domain
Photograph	• Highlight the ways that photographs document family events and activities.	Home and Family
Photograph	• Identify options for learning more about photography training (e.g., boys/girls clubs, community centers, school clubs/programs). • Name different types of photographs (e.g., candid, portraits, scenic, color, black and white).	Leisure Pursuits
Families	• Name community activities you and your family can participate in. • Identify community services you and your family use.	Community Involvement
Families	• List precautions you can take to prevent the spread of germs and illness from one person to another. • Describe activities you and your family do to maintain general good health.	Personal/Emotional Health

Subject Area:	Social Studies
Type of Material:	Textbook
Grade Level:	5th grade
Book Title/Page:	*People in Time and Place: Our Country*, page 563
Authors:	H. Bass
Publisher:	Silver Burdett Ginn
Copyright Date:	1991

People also exchanged mandarin oranges happily. The oranges are symbols of happiness and prosperity. Yang loved the New Year's celebration. It was her favorite holiday because it was a very happy time, and there was lots of merrymaking and good food.

After breakfast, Yang and her family started on their visits. Everywhere, happy people greeted them. Everyone said "Kong Hee Fatt Choy." That means "We wish you prosperity."

From *Reading Milestones: An Alternative Reading Program*, Level 6, Orange Reader 9 (2nd ed., p. 36), by S. P. Quigley, C. M. King, P. L. McAnally, and S. Rose, 1991, Austin, TX: PRO-ED. Copyright 1991 by PRO-ED, Inc. Reprinted with permission.

Content Referent	Possible Life Skills Topics	Adult Domain
Celebration	• List family celebrations other than the typical holidays.	Home and Family
Celebration	• Identify some neighborhood celebrations that occur throughout the year.	Leisure Pursuits
Symbols	• Identify symbols you see every day in your community (e.g., traffic signs, parking for drivers who are disabled, hospital signs, railroad signs, deer crossing).	Community Involvement
New Year's	• Name some New Year's resolutions that people make to improve their health.	Physical/Emotional Health

Subject Area:	Reading/English
Type of Material:	Textbook
Grade Level:	3rd grade
Book Title/Page:	*Reading Milestones*, Level 6, Orange Book 1 (2nd ed.), page 36
Authors:	S. P. Quigley, C. M. King, P. L. McAnally, and S. Rose
Publisher:	PRO-ED
Copyright Date:	1991

MIDDLE SCHOOL LEVEL EXAMPLES

LIGHT and VISION

Do you ever want a drink of water in the middle of the night? You grope for the flashlight with your hand in the dark room. Finally you find it, turn it on, and point the flashlight beam to find the door. The dresser is visible if you point the light beam at it, but as soon as you move the light toward the door, the dresser seems to disappear. The only objects you can see are the ones at which you point the flashlight beam.

Seeing any object requires light. Light may come from a flashlight, the light bulbs in your house, or from the sun. There are probably other sources of light in your home as well. Can you name them? How does light allow you to see the world around you? In this chapter, you'll learn about light and how it affects what you see.

▶ *In the activity on the next page, explore some characteristics of light and shadows.*

Did you ever wonder...

✓ **Why you can mix paints to get completely different colors?**

✓ **How long it takes for sunlight to travel to Earth?**

✓ **Why it's hard to distinguish different colors in moonlight?**

Before you begin to study about light and vision, think about these questions and answer them *in your Journal*. When you finish the chapter, compare your Journal write-up with what you have learned.

Content Referent	Possible Life Skills Topics	Adult Domain
Light	• Identify jobs that require special lighting.	Employment/Education
Paints	• Name jobs, other than painter, that use paint on a regular basis.	
Flashlight	• Identify safety reasons for having a flashlight. • Identify supplies needed to keep a flashlight in operating order. • Describe appropriate storage/maintenance of a flashlight.	Home and Family
Flashlight	• Highlight reasons to have a flashlight when you go into the forest or woods.	Leisure Pursuits
Vision	• List reasons to protect your eyes when working. • Identify ways in which you can protect your vision.	Physical/Emotional Health

Subject Area:	Science
Type of Material:	Textbook
Grade Level:	6th grade
Book Title/Page:	*Science Interactions*, page 52
Authors:	R. Aiuto, B. Aldridge, J. Ballinger, A. Barefoot, L. Crow, R. Feather, A. Kaskel, C. Kramer, E. Ortleb, S. Snyder, & P. Zitzewitz
Publisher:	Glencoe McGraw Hill
Copyright Date:	1995

Problem Solving
Using the Strategies

UNDERSTAND
ANALYZE DATA
PLAN
ESTIMATE
SOLVE
EXAMINE

LEARN ABOUT IT

On Friday afternoon, 8 friends agreed to call each other over the weekend. Each friend talked to every other friend once. How many phone calls were made?

To solve some problems, you may want to use more than one strategy. To solve this problem, you can use the strategies **Draw a Picture, Make a Table,** and **Look for a Pattern.**

You can begin by **drawing a picture** to represent friends and phone calls.

2 friends
1 call

3 friends
3 calls

4 friends
6 calls

Then you can **make a table** showing the number of friends and the number of phone calls and **look for a pattern.**

Number of friends	Number of calls
2	1 > up 2
3	3 > up 3
4	6 > up 4
5	10 > up 5
6	15 > up 6
7	21 > up 7
8	28

Twenty-eight phone calls were made.

TRY IT OUT

Solve. Use Draw a Picture, Make a Table or Look for a Pattern.

1. The Chess Club has 10 members. Each member wants to play one game with every other member. How many games need to be played?

2. Mimi is planting gazanias in a triangular plot. She put 1 gazania in the first row, 3 in the second row, 5 in the third, and so on. She planted 9 rows. How many gazanias did she plant?

Content Referent	Possible Life Skills Topics	Adult Domain
Phone	• Name jobs related to telecommunications.	Employment/Education
Gazanias	• List the responsibilities of having flowers in your home.	Home and Family
	• List the benefits of having flowers in your home.	
Gazanias	• Name the reasons why people have gardens.	Leisure Pursuits
	• Identify types of plants found in gardens.	
	• Identify the tasks associated with gardening.	
Phone	• Describe appropriate phone usage.	Personal Responsibility and Relationships

Subject Area:	Math
Type of Material:	Textbook
Grade Level:	7th grade
Book Title/Page:	*Addison-Wesley Mathematics,* page 170
Authors:	R. Eicholz, P.O. Daffer, R. Charles, S. Young, C. Barnett, C. Fleenor, S. Clemens, C. Thornton, A. Reeves, and J. Westley
Publisher:	Addison-Wesley Longman
Copyright Date:	1991

Tornadoes are a second kind of violent storm common to Louisiana. Their high winds can cause great damage, but they usually occur over a small area. Most of them form during the unsettled weather conditions of spring. The greatest number of tornadoes Louisiana has had in any one year was in 1974. In that year, Louisiana had 55 tornadoes!

Plant Life. The climate of a region directly affects what kind of plants can grow there. Louisiana's warm and wet climate encourages a wide variety of plant life. In the north, there are several types of pines, along with flowering trees and wild shrubs. In the alluvial areas, you will find cypress, oak, gum, and hickory trees. In the marshes, only a few hardwood trees grow. The marshes, however, support a vast array of wildflowers such as iris, lilies, and hibiscus.

Animal Life. The climate also affects the kinds of animals found in an area. Louisiana's warm, wet climate makes it a good home for deer, rabbits, weasels, nutria, raccoons, muskrats, and alligators. The marshes of Louisiana support a great number of ducks, turkeys, and quail. Many birds winter in Louisiana. It is estimated that 25% of the ducks in the United States are in Louisiana during the month of January.

Louisiana's climate is determined by several factors. One factor is the state's location in the mild temperate zone. Another factor is the Gulf of Mexico. The difference in temperature between the land and water influences Louisiana's weather. Also, moisture from the Gulf of Mexico is absorbed by the air and falls on Louisiana as rain.

Louisiana's subtropical climate contributes to its uniqueness and its quality of life. The state's warm weather makes it an ideal site for outdoor activities and festivals.

Alligators

Content Referent	Possible Life Skills Topics	Adult Domain
Tornado	• Describe the differences between a meteorologist and a weather person. • Identify training needed to be a weather person or meteorologist.	Employment/Education
Damage	• Name different types of insurance you should have in case of storm damage to your home.	Home and Family
Flowers	• Identify the students who have a garden at home. • Name different types of flowers grown in home gardens.	Leisure Pursuits
Festivals	• Name the types of festivals in your community or school. • Identify the purpose of each festival. • Describe how you can participate in these festivals.	Community Involvement
Tornadoes	• Describe what you do when there is a tornado warning.	Physical/Emotional Health
Festivals	• Identify the responsibilities of being a festival volunteer (e.g., being on time, task completion, shift completion). • List the perks of being a festival volunteer.	Personal Responsibility and Relationships

Subject Area:	Social Studies
Type of Material:	Textbook
Grade Level:	8th grade
Book Title/Page:	*Louisiana: A Study in Diversity*, page 22
Authors:	H. Dethloff & A.E. Begnaud
Publisher:	Steck-Vaughn
Copyright Date:	1992

My mind wandered, recalling previous annual gatherings at Grandma's house. Memories of the fresh, clean smell of her kitchen replaced the stale, greasy stink of gasoline and oil. Ham hocks and collard greens stewed on the stove alongside a large kettle of black-eyed peas. I closed my eyes and could see the homemade breads and the freshly baked yam and apple pies. My cousins and I would run in and out of the kitchen trying to snitch a piece of pie or grab a chicken wing. Grandma would shoo us away with her apron, saying, "Just you wait, child. There's plenty for those who wait." And then she would give each of us a cookie to hold us over "till the food's ready."

Then there was Gramps, always telling us wonderful stories. He would seat himself on a favorite wide, old tree stump in the backyard, and all the grandchildren would gather around him. Gramps would take his time puffing on his corn-cob pipe and think awhile. He would count noses, twenty-four in all. When all of the grandchildren were quiet, he would start telling the stories of the Old South. He'd tell us about our kin—especially his daddy, our great-grandfather—and about how he worked as a slave for some rich white folks. That's how he got the farm. He told stories of famous people like Martin Luther King, Roy Wilkens, and Jackie Robinson. These were Gramps's heroes. They worked for peace and equal rights for all people. He also told us stories we didn't want to hear—stories about slavery, prejudice, and discrimination. I didn't understand those stories then. I was too young to know that skin color made people different.

From *Reading Bridge, Mosaic*, Level 1, Book 1 (p. 157), by S. P. Quigley, P. V. Paul, P. L. McAnally, S. Rose, and J. Payne, 1989, Austin, TX: PRO-ED. Copyright 1989 by PRO-ED, Inc. Reprinted with permission.

Content Referent	Possible Life Skills Topics	Adult Domain
Grandfather	• Identify jobs that are related to working with older adults.	Employment/Education
Heroes	• Identify people in your community who have had a positive impact on the community.	Community Involvement
	• Describe volunteer experiences that you have had that have had a positive impact on the community.	
Grandfather	• List some health difficulties that older adults may experience.	Physical/Emotional Health
Equal Rights	• Describe Equal Rights. • Identify your responsibilities concerning Equal Rights.	Personal Responsibility and Relationships

Subject Area:	Reading
Type of Material:	Textbook
Grade Level:	Middle School
Book Title/Page:	*Mosaic*, page 157
Authors:	S. P. Quigley, P. V. Paul, P. L. McAnally, S. Rose, & J. Payne
Publisher:	PRO-ED
Copyright Date:	1989

Chapter 2

The Carpetbag

I stuffed a shirt into my old carpetbag and said good-bye to the city of Manhatto. I arrived in New Bedford on a cold, windy, and icy Saturday in December. I was too late for a boat ride to Nantucket, the great sailing port of America. I had to wait until Monday before I could go there. Then, I would go on my great whaling voyage. But for now, I needed some food and a place to sleep. I had little money and knew I had few choices, if any.

I walked for many blocks and looked for shelter from the cold. I saw lots of inns, but they were all too expensive. My steps led me to the waterfront. I found the cheapest places in that part of town. I also found blocks of blackness. A few candles gave the only light. But I had to pass inn after inn because they looked too expensive.

Moving on, I came to a dim light near the docks. The sign over the door said "The Spouter Inn—Peter Coffin." The place looked quiet. The house was old and *run-down*.

This looked like a good place to stay. If I was lucky, they might even serve coffee. It didn't really matter. I was tired and had ice on my feet. I had run out of choices. So I decided to go into the inn and see it on the inside.

Content Referent	Possible Life Skills Topics	Adult Domain
Inn	• Identify employment opportunities in the hotel industry (e.g., desk clerk, manager, bellhop, concierge, room service, food preparation). • Identify the required education or training for these employment opportunities.	Employment/Education
Inn	• List different types of lodgings (e.g., hotel, motel, hostel, YMCA, campgrounds). • Identify the advance preparations or information needed prior to arriving at a hotel (e.g., reservations, room availability, room rates).	Leisure Pursuits
Inn	• List responsibilities you accept once you have checked into a hotel (e.g., notify the hotel if the room condition is not correct, hotel rules, know the checkout time).	Personal Responsibility and Relationships

Subject Area:	Literature
Type of Material:	Novel
Grade Level:	Middle School
Book Title/Page:	*Moby Dick*, page 2
Author:	H. Melville (Adapted by M. Montroy)
Publisher:	PRO-ED
Copyright Date:	1991

HIGH SCHOOL LEVEL EXAMPLES

■CROSS CURRENTS■

Native American Voices Today

The coming of white settlers to North America in the seventeenth century resulted in almost complete destruction of the Native American societies there. Whole tribes were nearly wiped out in battles or by diseases brought by the Europeans. Survivors were forced off their lands and herded indiscriminately into designated reservations, where many more died. Those left were soon surrounded and controlled by a society they had little knowledge of and no place in.

The land on which each tribe lived was central and sacred to their life. It fed and clothed them. Just as important, the land contained the bones of their ancestors and therefore the knowledge and power of the past, of the Old Ones. Separated from this power and obliged to learn the white man's ways to survive, Native Americans were in danger of losing forever their identity, language, and traditions. Fortunately, through dedicated work by determined tribal members and some enlightened whites, the Native Americans and the United States have not completely lost this heritage.

A REBIRTH OF NATIVE AMERICAN LITERATURE

Recently, Native American voices are once again heard in the land. Some are angry, some sorrowful, others wryly comic—all are powerful. Native Americans are again telling stories and composing poems of their past and present, attempting to create connections between them. Many of their books have become best-sellers.

The one book most credited with beginning the current "rebirth" of Native American literature is N. Scott Momaday's Pulitzer Prize-winning novel, *House Made of Dawn*, published in 1969. Momaday (page 922) was quickly followed by such writers as Leslie Marmon Silko (Laguna Pueblo), Simon Ortiz (Acoma Pueblo), and James Welch (Blackfeet/Gros Ventre).

All these writers vividly portray the struggle of Native Americans to keep hold of their past, live in the present, and create a future. None of the authors romanticize either the past or the present, as many nineteenth-century writers did. The characters in their novels, like themselves, are often only part Native American and must relearn what their grandparents grew up knowing. At the same time, they are living in a modern society where traditional ways of living do not seem possible.

Louise Erdrich

The tragic—and comic—elements of these characters' lives are vividly portrayed by author Louise Erdrich. Erdrich is a member of the Turtle Mountain Chippewa Reservation in North Dakota, where her grandparents lived. She now lives in New Hampshire with her husband, Michael Dorris, a professor of Native American literature at Dartmouth College.

Erdrich has published three novels, two volumes of poetry, and numerous short stories. Her novels are set in the vicinity of the Chippewa territory and are peopled with sev-

Content Referent	Possible Life Skills Topics	Adult Domain
Diseases	• List the jobs related to disease treatment and prevention.	Employment/Education
Traditions	• Identify the traditions your family participates in during the year.	Leisure Pursuits
Native American	• Identify any Native Americans that may have inhabited the land surrounding your community.	Community Involvement
Diseases	• Identify illnesses or diseases that are communicable. • Identify communicable diseases that are found in developing countries.	Physical/Emotional Health

Subject Area:	Literature
Type of Material:	Textbook
Grade Level:	Secondary
Book Title/Page:	*Literature: The American Experience*, page 31
Publisher:	Prentice-Hall
Copyright Date:	1994

they are placed carefully on the surface, they remain there. A close look at the water surface shows that the needle or razor blade is supported in a hollow in the water surface, as seen in Figure 7-12. *The water acts as though it has a thin, flexible surface film.* The weight of the needle or razor blade is counterbalanced by the upward force that is exerted by the surface film. This property of liquids is due to *surface tension.*

All liquids show surface tension. Mercury has a very high surface tension. In many liquids the surface film is not as strong as that of water or mercury. Part of the cleaning action of detergents is due to their ability to lower the surface tension of water. This makes it possible for the water and detergent to penetrate more readily between the fibers of the articles being cleaned and the dirt particles.

Since particles in a liquid attract similar liquid particles that are nearby, they move as close together as possible. Hence the surface will tend to have a minimum area. The effect of this attraction is to make the liquid behave as if it were contained in a stretched elastic skin. The *tension* in this "skin" is the *surface tension.* When a force acts on a liquid surface film and distorts that film, the cohesion of the liquid molecules exerts an equal and opposite force that tends to restore the horizontal surface. Thus the weight of a supported needle produces a depression in the water surface film that increases the area of the film. In order to restore the surface of the liquid to its original horizontal condition, the cohesion of the water molecules exerts a counterbalancing upward force on the needle.

Surface tension produces contraction forces in liquid films. A liquid film has two free surfaces on which molecules are subject to an unbalanced force toward the inside of the film. Thus both free surfaces tend to assume a minimum area. The contraction of the film can be demonstrated by the device shown in Figure 7-13. A wire ring containing a loop of thread is dipped into a soap solution causing a film to form across the ring. If the film inside the loop of thread is broken with a hot wire the unbroken film outside the loop contracts and pulls the thread equally on all sides to form a circle.

Surface tension causes a free liquid to assume a spherical shape. A free liquid is one that is not acted upon by any external force. This condition can be approximated by small drops of mercury on a table top, as shown in Figure 7-14. A sphere has the smallest surface area for a given volume. The unbalanced force acting on liquid surface molecules tends to pull them toward the center of the liquid, reducing the surface area and causing the liquid to

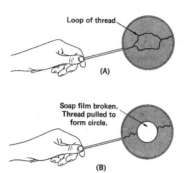

Figure 7-13. In (A), a soap film covers the entire area inside the ring. When the film inside the loop of thread is broken (B), the film outside the loop contracts and pulls the thread into a circle.

Content Referent	Possible Life Skills Topics	Adult Domain
Mercury	• Identify your rights and responsibilities in the event of a chemical or hazardous material spill.	Personal Responsibility and Relationships
Detergent	• Describe how you can make bubbles from a mixture of detergent and water.	Leisure Pursuits
Mercury	• List the steps your community follows in the event of a chemical or hazardous material spill.	Community Involvement

Subject Area:	Physics
Type of Material:	Science Textbook
Grade Level:	Secondary
Book Title/Page:	*Modern Physics*, page 153
Authors:	J. E. Williams, F. E. Trinklein, & H. C. Metcalfe
Publisher:	Holt, Rinehart and Winston
Copyright Date:	1984

3 Emergence of Islam

READ TO UNDERSTAND

☐ **How Muhammad founded the religion of Islam.**

☐ **What the beliefs of Muslims are.**

☐ **Why Islam spread so rapidly.**

☐ *Vocabulary:* hejira, mosque, caliph.

The 4,000 riders raised clouds of dust for miles around. The Arab army followed the much-worn path of Alexander the Great and other conquerors southward along the coast of Palestine into Egypt. Outside of Cairo, they halted. Inside the city walls, the Byzantines had a garrison of 50,000 soldiers.

The Arab general Amr-ibn-al-As had no siege machines, no ships, and no source of new recruits. But he was confident of victory. Within a year, Amr could send the news: "Allahua akbar" ("God is most great"). Cairo, one of the greatest cities of the Byzantine Empire, had fallen.

Cairo was just one of many cities to fall to the armies of Islam during the 600s. The new religion of Islam had united the peoples of Arabia. Like Judaism and Christianity, Islam had a profound impact on history. Within 100 years after it was founded, its followers, known as Muslims, had built an empire that was larger than the Roman Empire at its height.

GEOGRAPHIC SETTING
Arabia

Arabia, the birthplace of Islam, is the largest peninsula in the world. It is a hilly, arid land dotted with occasional oases—fertile areas with enough water to support trees and plants. As great civilizations rose and fell in the Fertile Crescent to the north, the Arabs developed a way of life well adapted to the desert conditions of their homeland.

Most Arabs were nomads who herded goats and camels. They were loosely organized into tribes with strong codes of honor. Their poets praised the fierce independence of their warriors. Yet this independence led to frequent feuds that prevented unity among the different Arab tribes.

Arabia was a vital link that connected the Mediterranean world, Asia, and the east coast of Africa. Some Arabs, who lived in towns along the Red Sea, traded with the Greco-Roman world as well as with India, China, and Africa.

Mecca, a town near the Red Sea, prospered as a trading and religious center. Pilgrims traveled to Mecca to worship at the Kaaba, a sacred shrine that housed images of all the Arab gods. The Kaaba also housed a black stone—probably a meteorite—that the Arabs believed was sent from heaven. ■

Muhammad: Founder of Islam

Muhammad was born in Mecca about 570. His parents died when he was still a child, and he was raised by relatives who belonged to a poor but prominent Arab family. Little else is known about Muhammad's early life.

At age 25, Muhammad married Khadija (kah DEE jah), a wealthy widow who ran her late husband's business. With Khadija's help, Muhammad became a successful merchant. Yet he was troubled by the violence and treachery he saw in the world. He often went into the desert to pray. When he prayed, Muhammad believed that the angel Gabriel spoke to him, saying that God had chosen Muhammad as his prophet. Muhammad's duty, said the angel, was to proclaim that Allah, or God, was the one and only God.

At first, only Khadija and a few friends believed Muhammad. The merchants and innkeepers of Mecca opposed him. They thought that his teaching about one God would destroy their income from Arab pilgrims. Threatened with death, Muhammad and his followers fled Mecca in 622. They were welcomed at Yathrib, a rival commercial town on the Red Sea. Yathrib, later renamed Medina, became known as the City of the Prophet.

Muslims call Muhammad's journey from Mecca to Medina the **hejira** (hih JĪ ruh), or departure. The year 622 was made the first year of the Muslim calendar. The hejira marked a turning point in Muhammad's life. In Medina, he gained power as both a religious and political leader.

Content Referent	Possible Life Skills Topics	Adult Domain
Recruits	• What is the purpose of schools and employers recruiting individuals? • Where does this occur and how do you find out about it? • Describe how you prepare for a job or college fair. What should you take?	Employment/Education
Tribe	• Name the members that make up your family at home or school. • Discuss what features or symbols can be associated with different tribes.	Home and Family
Tribe	• List various tribes or groups in your community, and their purpose.	Community Involvement
Feuds	• Describe how you manage stress and anxiety when involved in a feud or conflict?	Physical/Emotional Health
Feuds	• Discuss effective and appropriate communication skills. • Discuss how you feel when you receive negative or positive feedback from others. • Discuss the importance of compromising and accepting conflict resolution assistance.	Personal Responsibility and Relationships

Subject Area:	World History
Type of Material:	Textbook
Grade Level:	Secondary
Book Title/Page:	*World History; Patterns of Civilization*, page 231
Author:	B. Beers
Publisher:	Prentice-Hall
Copyright Date:	1991

To make an orthographic projection into an isometric drawing, we fold the top, front, and side together. The base of the box becomes angled, but vertical lines remain vertical, parallel lines remain parallel, and congruence is preserved.

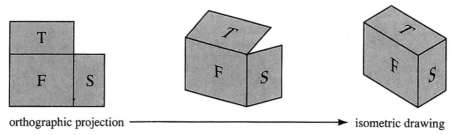

orthographic projection ⟶ isometric drawing

To illustrate, we shall make an isometric drawing of the solid whose orthographic projection is shown below. Visible edges and intersections are shown as solid lines. Hidden edges are shown as dashed lines.

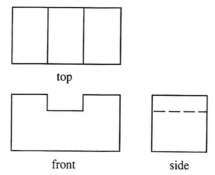

Begin by drawing three rays with a common endpoint such that one ray is vertical and the other two rays are 30° off of horizontal. Mark off the lengths of the front, side, and height of the solid. By drawing congruent segments and by showing parallel edges as parallel in the figure, you can finish the isometric drawing. The figures that follow suggest the procedure.

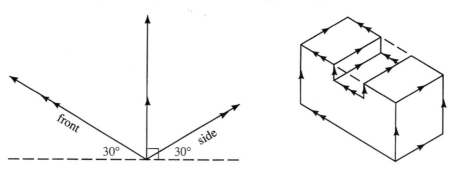

Industry requires millions of drawings similar to these each year. The drafters who make these drawings professionally combine the knowledge of parallel lines with the skills of using a compass, a protractor, and a ruler. More recently, drafters make drawings like these using a computer and a special printer.

Content Referent	Possible Life Skills Topics	Adult Domain
Drafters	• Identify training programs in your area where one can get training in drafting.	Employment/Education
Drawing	• Discuss home situations where an understanding of isometric drawings is important.	Home and Family
Isometric	• Describe isometric exercises.	Physical/Emotional Health
	• Highlight how they can be part of a healthy lifestyle.	

Subject Area:	Geometry
Type of Material:	Textbook
Grade Level:	Secondary
Book Title/Page:	*Geometry*, page 91
Authors:	R. Jurgensen, R. Brown, & J. Jurgensen
Publisher:	Houghton-Mifflin
Copyright Date:	1994

A **formula** is an equation that states a relationship between two or more variables. The variables usually represent physical or geometric quantities. For example, the formula $h = -16t^2 + vt$ gives the height h (in feet) of a launched object t seconds after firing with initial velocity v (in ft/s). Given values for all but one of the variables in a formula, you can find the value of the remaining variable.

Example 3 A model rocket launched with initial velocity v reaches a height of 40 ft after 2.5 s. Find v.

Solution Substitute the given values of the variables.

$$h = -16t^2 + vt$$
$$40 = -16(2.5)^2 + v(2.5)$$
$$40 = -100 + 2.5v$$
$$140 = 2.5v$$
$$v = 56 \text{ (ft/s)} \quad \textbf{\textit{Answer}}$$

When you solve a formula or equation for a certain variable, you can think of all the other variables as **constants,** that is, as fixed numbers. Then solve by the usual methods.

Example 4 The volume V of a pyramid with height h and square base with sides s is given by the formula $V = \frac{1}{3}s^2h$. Solve this formula for h.

Solution You need to express h in terms of the other variables. That is, you need to get h alone on one side of the equation.

$$V = \frac{1}{3}s^2h$$
$$3(V) = 3\left(\frac{1}{3}s^2h\right)$$
$$3V = s^2h$$
$$\frac{3V}{s^2} = \frac{s^2h}{s^2} \quad \text{(Assume } s \neq 0.\text{)}$$
$$h = \frac{3V}{s^2} \quad \textbf{\textit{Answer}}$$

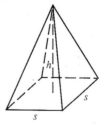

Content Referent	Possible Life Skills Topics	Adult Domain
Solve	• Identify various ways everyday problems can be solved in a family (e.g., what to have for dinner, what to watch on TV, where to go on vacations).	Home and Family
Variables	• Identify the variables involved in various individual or group indoor or outdoor activities (e.g., transportation, equipment, finances, number of people involved).	Leisure Pursuits
	• Identify the variables involved in attending various community or neighborhood activities (e.g., cost, transportation, purpose).	Personal Responsibility and Relationships
Variables	• Describe variables involved in establishing and maintaining friendships.	
	• Identify variables involved in improving one's academic achievement.	

Subject Area:	Algebra and Trigonometry
Type of Material:	Textbook
Grade Level:	Secondary
Book Title/Page:	*Algebra and Trigonometry: Structure and Method, Book 2*, page 39
Authors:	R. Brown, M. Dolciani, R. Sorgenfrey, & R. Kane
Publisher:	Houghton Mifflin
Copyright Date:	1997

Appendix A
Major Life Demands

Domain	Subdomain	Life Demands
Employment/ Education	General Job Skills	seeking and securing a job
		learning job skills
		maintaining one's job
		understanding fundamental and legal issues
	General Education/ Training Considerations	knowing about education/training options
		gaining entry to post-secondary education/training settings (higher education, adult education, community education, trade/technical schools, military service)
		finding financial support
		utilizing academic and system survival skills (e.g., study skills, organizational skills, and time management)
		requesting employment services when needed (e.g., VR (Vocational Rehabilitation), unemployment)
		accessing support services of training setting
	Employment Setting	recognizing job duties and responsibilities
		exhibiting appropriate work habits/behavior
		getting along with employer and co-workers
		understanding company policies (e.g., fringe benefits, wages, sick/personal leave, advancement procedures)
		understanding take-home pay/deductions
		managing employment-related expenses (travel, clothes, dues)
		understanding OSHA regulations
	Career Refinement and Re-evaluation	revitalizing career choice
		exploring alternative career options
		pursuing career change
Home and Family	Home Management	setting up household operations (e.g., initiating utilities)
		arranging furniture and equipment
		identifying and implementing security provisions and safety procedures

(continues)

Domain	Subdomain	Life Demands
Home and Family *(continued)*	Home Management *(continued)*	cleaning dwelling
		maintaining and landscaping a yard
		laundering and maintaining clothes and household items
		performing/contracting for home repairs/improvements and regular maintenance
		storing household items
		maintaining automobile(s) and equipment, appliances, etc.
		reacting to environmental dangers (e.g., pollution, extreme weather conditions)
	Financial Management	creating a general financial plan (e.g., savings, investments, retirement)
		maintaining a budget
		using banking services
		paying bills
		establishing a good credit rating
		purchasing day-to-day items (clothes, food, etc.)
		renting an apartment
		selecting and buying a house (building new/purchasing existing)
		making major purchases (e.g., auto)
		determining payment options for major purchases (cash, credit, layaway, debit card, finance plan, etc.)
		preparing and paying taxes
		buying insurance
		purchasing specialty items throughout the year (e.g., birthday gifts, Christmas gifts, etc.)
		planning for long-term financial needs (e.g., major purchases, children's education)
		obtaining government assistance when needed (e.g., Medicare, food stamps, student loans)
	Family Life	preparing for marriage, family
		maintaining physical/emotional health of family members
		maintaining family harmony
		scheduling and managing daily, weekly, monthly, yearly family events (e.g., appointments, social events, leisure/recreational pursuits)
		planning and preparing meals (menu, buying food, ordering take-out food, dining out)
		arranging for/providing day care (children or older relatives)
		managing incoming/outgoing mail

(continues)

Domain	Subdomain	Life Demands
Home and Family *(continued)*	Child Rearing	acquiring realistic information about raising children
		preparing for pregnancy and childbirth
		understanding childhood development (physical, emotional, cognitive, language)
		managing children's behavior
		preparing for out-of-home experiences (e.g., day care, school)
		helping children with school-related needs
		hiring and training in-home babysitter
Leisure Pursuits	Indoor Activities	playing table/electronic games (e.g., cards, board games, puzzles, Nintendo, arcades, etc.)
		performing individual physical activities (e.g., weight training, aerobics, dance, swimming, martial arts)
		participating in group physical activities (e.g., racquetball, basketball)
		engaging in individual hobbies and crafts (e.g., reading, handicrafts, sewing, collecting)
	Outdoor Activities	performing individual physical activities (e.g., jogging, golf, bicycling, swimming, hiking, backpacking, fishing)
		participating in group physical activities (e.g., softball, football, basketball, tennis)
		engaging in general recreational activities (e.g., camping, sightseeing, picnicking)
	Community/ Neighborhood Activities	going to various ongoing neighborhood events (e.g., garage sales, block parties, BBQs)
		attending special events (e.g., fairs, trade shows, carnivals, parades, festivals)
	Travel	preparing to go on a trip (e.g., destination, transportation arrangements, hotel/motel arrangements, packing, preparations for leaving home)
		dealing with the realities of travel via air, ground, or water
	Entertainment	engaging in in-home activities (e.g., TV, videos, music)
		attending out-of-home events (e.g., theaters, spectator sports, concerts, performances, art shows)
		going to socially oriented events (e.g., restaurants, parties, nightclubs) and other social events
Community Involvement	Citizenship	understanding legal rights
		exhibiting civic responsibility
		voting in elections
		understanding tax obligations
		obeying laws and ordinances

(continues)

Domain	Subdomain	Life Demands
Community Involvement *(continued)*	Citizenship *(continued)*	serving on a jury
		understanding judicial procedures (e.g., due process, criminal/civil courts, legal documents)
		attending public hearings
		creating change in the community (e.g., petition drives)
	Community Awareness	being aware of social issues affecting community
		knowing major events at the local, regional, national, world levels
		using mass media (TV, radio, newspaper)
		understanding all sides of public opinion on community issues
		recognizing and acting on fraudulent practices
	Services/Resources	knowing about the wide range of services available in a specific community
		using all levels of government agencies (tax office, driver's license, permits, consumer agencies)
		accessing public transportation (trains, buses, subways, ferries, etc.)
		accessing private services (humane society, cable services, utilities [phone, water, electric, sewage, garbage])
		accessing emergency services/resources (police, EMS, hospital, fire, civil defense)
		accessing agencies that provide special services (advocacy centers)
		securing legal representation (e.g., lawyer reference service)
Physical/Emotional Health	Physical	living a healthy lifestyle
		planning a nutritional diet
		exercising regularly as part of lifestyle
		having regular physical/dental checkups
		understanding illnesses and medical/dental needs across age levels
		using proper dental hygiene/dental care
		preventing illness and accidents
		recognizing health risks
		recognizing signs of medical/dental problems
		reacting to medical emergencies
		administering simple first aid
		using medications
		providing treatment for chronic health problems
		recognizing and accommodating physical changes associated with aging
		recognizing and dealing with substance use/abuse

(continues)

Domain	Subdomain	Life Demands
Physical/Emotional Health *(continued)*	Emotional	understanding emotional needs across age levels
		recognizing signs of emotional needs
		managing life changes
		managing stress
		dealing with adversity and depression
		dealing with anxiety
		coping with separation/death of family members and friends
		understanding emotional dimensions of sexuality
		seeking personal counseling
Personal Responsibility and Relationships	Personal Confidence/ Understanding	recognizing one's strengths and weaknesses
		appreciating one's accomplishments
		identifying ways to maintain or achieve a positive self-concept
		reacting appropriately to the positive or negative feedback of others
		using appropriate communication skills
		following one's religious beliefs
	Goal Setting	evaluating one's values
		identifying and achieving personal goals and aspirations
		exercising problem-solving/decision-making skills
		becoming independent and self-directed
	Self-Improvement	pursuing personal interests
		conducting self-evaluation
		seeking continuing education
		improving scholastic abilities
		displaying appropriate personal interaction skills
		maintaining personal appearance
	Relationships	getting along with others
		establishing and maintaining friendships
		developing intimate relations
		deciding upon potential spouse or partner
		being sensitive to the needs of others
		communicating praise or criticism to others
		being socially perceptive (e.g., recognizing contextual clues)
		dealing with conflict
		nurturing healthy child/parent interactions
		solving marital problems
	Personal Expression	sharing personal feelings, experiences, concerns, desires with other people
		writing personal correspondence (e.g., letters, notes, greeting cards)

From *Life Skills Instruction for All Students with Special Needs: A Practical Guide for Integrating Real-Life Content into the Curriculum* (pp. 16–19), by M. E. Cronin and J. R. Patton, 1993, Austin, TX: PRO-ED. Copyright 1993 by PRO-ED, Inc. Reprinted with permission.

Appendix B
Life-Centered Career Education Subcompetencies

Life Centered Career Education Competencies (Revised 1/87)

Curriculum Area	Competency	Subcompetency: The student will be able to:	
Daily Living Skills	1. Managing Personal Finances	1. Count money & make correct change	2. Make responsible expenditures
	2. Selecting & Managing a Household	7. Maintain home exterior/interior	8. Use basic appliances and tools
	3. Caring for Personal Needs	12. Demonstrate knowledge of physical fitness, nutrition & weight	13. Exhibit proper grooming & hygiene
	4. Raising Children & Meeting Marriage Responsibilities	17. Demonstrate physical care for raising children	18. Know psychological aspects of raising children
	5. Buying, Preparing & Consuming Food	20. Purchase food	21. Clean food preparation areas
	6. Buying & Caring for Clothing	26. Wash/clean clothing	27. Purchase clothing
	7. Exhibiting Responsible Citizenship	29. Demonstrate knowledge of civil rights & responsibilities	30. Know nature of local, state & federal governments
	8. Utilizing Recreational Facilities & Engaging in Leisure	33. Demonstrate knowledge of available community resources	34. Choose & plan activities
	9. Getting Around the Community	38. Demonstrate knowledge of traffic rules & safety	39. Demonstrate knowledge & use of various means of transportation
Personal-Social Skills	10. Achieving Self Awareness	42. Identify physical & psychological needs	43. Identify interests & abilities
	11. Acquiring Self Confidence	46. Express feelings of self-worth	47. Describe other's perception of self
	12. Achieving Socially Responsible Behavior	51. Develop respect for the rights & properties of others	52. Recognize authority & follow instructions
	13. Maintaining Good Interpersonal Skills	56. Demonstrate listening & responding skills	57. Establish & maintain close relationships
	14. Achieving Independence	59. Strive toward self-actualization	60. Demonstrate self-organization
	15. Making Adequate Decisions	62. Locate & utilize sources of assistance	63. Anticipate consequences
	16. Communicating with Others	67. Recognize & respond to emergency situations	68. Communicate with understanding
Occupational Guidance and Preparation	17. Knowing & Exploring Occupational Possibilities	70. Identify remunerative aspects of work	71. Locate sources of occupational & training information
	18. Selecting & Planning Occupational Choices	76. Make realistic occupational choices	77. Identify requirements of appropriate & available jobs
	19. Exhibiting Appropriate Work Habits & Behavior	81. Follow directions & observe regulations	82. Recognize importance of attendance & punctuality
	20. Seeking, Securing & Maintaining Employment	88. Search for a job	89. Apply for a job
	21. Exhibiting Sufficient Physical-Manual Skills	94. Demonstrate stamina & endurance	95. Demonstrate satisfactory balance & coordination
	22. Obtaining Specific Occupational Skills		

3. Keep basic financial records	4. Calculate & pay taxes	5. Use credit responsibly	6. Use banking services	
9. Select adequate housing	10. Set up household	11. Maintain home grounds		
14. Dress appropriately	15. Demonstrate knowledge of common illness, prevention & treatment	16. Practice personal safety		
19. Demonstrate marriage responsibilities				
22. Store food	23. Prepare meals	24. Demonstrate appropriate eating habits	25. Plan/eat balanced meals	
28. Iron, mend & store clothing				
31. Demonstrate knowledge of the law & ability to follow the law	32. Demonstrate knowledge of citizen rights & responsibilities			
35. Demonstrate knowledge of the value of recreation	36. Engage in group & individual activities	37. Plan vacation time		
40. Find way around the community	41. Drive a car			
44. Identify emotions	45. Demonstrate knowledge of physical self			
48. Accept & give praise	49. Accept & give criticism	50. Develop confidence in oneself		
53. Demonstrate appropriate behavior in public places	54. Know important character traits	55. Recognize personal roles		
58. Make & maintain friendships				
61. Demonstrate awareness of how one's behavior affects others				
64. Develop & evaluate alternatives	65. Recognize nature of a problem	66. Develop goal seeking behavior		
69. Know subtleties of communication				
72. Identify personal values met through work	73. Identify societal values met through work	74. Classify jobs into occupational categories	75. Investigate local occupational & training opportunities	
78. Identify occupational aptitudes	79. Identify major occupational interests	80. Identify major occupational needs		
83. Recognize importance of supervision	84. Demonstrate knowledge of occupational safely	85. Work with others	86. Meet demands for quality work	87. Work at a satisfactory rate
90. Interview for a job	91. Know how to maintain post-school occupational adjustment	92. Demonstrate knowledge of competitive standards	93. Know how to adjust to changes in employment	
96. Demonstrate manual dexterity	97. Demonstrate sensory discrimination			

There are no specific subcompetencies as they depend on skill being taught

Note. From *Life-Centered Career Education: A Competency-Based Approach* (5th ed., pp. 10–11) by D. E. Brolin, 1997, Reston, VA: The Council for Exceptional Children.

Appendix C
Life Skills Infusion Forms

Life Skills Infusion Planning Guide

Note: This planning guide is recommended for use when identifying content in existing curricular materials that can be linked to life skills topics.

Subject Area _____ **Material** _____

Content Referent	Possible Life Skills Topics	Notes

Life Skills Infusion Planning Form

Subject Area: _____

Type of Material: _____

Grade Level: _____

Book Title/Page: _____

Author(s): _____

Publisher: _____

Copyright Date: _____

Domain	Reference Point	Life Skill Topic

Appendix D
Practice Exercises

Families should practice fire prevention at home because most fires happen in homes. Careless smoking habits and the careless use of matches are responsible for some fires. Old electrical wiring and equipment start some fires, too. Grease on stoves and carelessness with fireplaces are responsible for fires, also.

From *Reading Milestones: An Alternative Reading Program*, Level 6, Orange Reader 9 (2nd ed., p. 13), by S. P. Quigley, C. M. King, P. L. McAnally, and S. Rose, 1991, Austin, TX: PRO-ED. Copyright 1991 by PRO-ED, Inc. Reprinted with permission.

Life Skills Infusion Planning Guide

Note: This planning guide is recommended for use when identifying content in existing curricular materials that can be linked to life skills topics.

Subject Area _____ **Material** _____

Content Referent	Possible Life Skills Topics	Notes

WAVES

Reflection may be partial or complete depending on the nature of the reflecting boundary. If there is no boundary mechanism for extracting energy from the wave, all the energy incident with the wave is reflected back with it.

When a surface wave in the ripple tank encounters the straight barrier, which is a rigid vertical bulkhead, the vertical transverse component of the wave is unrestrained. The wave crest is reflected *as a crest*, and the trough is reflected *as a trough*. The surface wave is reflected without a change in phase. *A boundary that allows unrestrained displacement of the particles of a medium reflects waves with no change in the direction of the displacement, which is equivalent to no change in phase.* The bulkhead acts as a *free-end* or *open-end* termination to the wave medium.

Suppose we send a transverse pulse traveling along a stretched string of which the far end is free. Having such a string presents no problem in a "thought" experiment. In practice, the free-ended termination might be approximated as shown in Figure 10-19. To the extent that the termination is frictionless, the end of the string is free to move in the plane of the pulse.

After arriving at the free end of the string, the pulse is reflected as shown in Figure 10-19. Observe that it has not been inverted. Displacement of the particles of the string is in the same direction as that for the incident pulse. During the time interval that the pulse is arriving at the free end of the string and the reflected pulse is leaving it, the combined effect of the two pulses causes the free end to experience twice the displacement as from either pulse alone. *Reflection at the free-end termination of a medium occurs without a change in phase.*

Now suppose we clamp the far end of the string in a fixed position and send a transverse pulse toward this termination. See Figure 10-20. When the pulse arrives at the fixed end, it applies an upward force to the clamp. An equal but opposite reaction force is applied to the string generating a reflected pulse that is inverted with respect to the incident pulse. *Reflection at the fixed termination of a medium occurs with a reversal of the direction of the displacement, or a phase shift of 180°.* In general, we may conclude that *a boundary that restrains the displacement of the particles of a medium reflects waves inverted in phase.*

Some examples of reflecting terminations for different kinds of wave disturbances are given in Table 10-1. The first three systems listed summarize the phase relations discussed in this section.

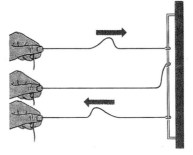

Figure 10-19. Reflection of a pulse at the "free" end of a taut string. The string is shown terminated in a "frictionless" ring that allows the end segment unrestrained displacement in the plane of the pulse.

Life Skills Infusion Planning Guide

Note: This planning guide is recommended for use when identifying content in existing curricular materials that can be linked to life skills topics.

Subject Area _____   **Material** _____

Content Referent	Possible Life Skills Topics	Notes

Problem Solving
Deciding When to Estimate

UNDERSTAND
FIND DATA
PLAN
ESTIMATE
SOLVE
CHECK

LEARN ABOUT IT

When you solve problems, you must decide if you need an exact answer or an estimate. When you estimate, you are finding **about how many.**

Suppose you start a lemonade stand. You need to compute your cost per glass, how much profit you want, and how much to charge per glass. How much will people buy?

You need to find out how much it will cost you to make 1 glass of lemonade so that you will know how much to charge.

> I can estimate the cost per glass since the size of each glass will not be exact.

You need to charge a customer for 2 large glasses and 3 small glasses.

> I need an exact answer when I charge my customers.

You must understand the situation in the problem before you can decide if you need an exact answer or if an estimate will be enough to answer the question.

TRY IT OUT

Think about the lemonade stand situation. Decide if you need an exact answer or an estimate.

1. You figure the change from a $5.00 bill after a purchase.

2. You figure how many glasses of lemonade you can get from 3 full pitchers of lemonade.

3. You tell a friend how much lemonade you sold.

4. You want to figure a fair price for a large glass of lemonade.

Life Skills Infusion Planning Guide

Note: This planning guide is recommended for use when identifying content in existing curricular materials that can be linked to life skills topics.

Subject Area _____ **Material** _____

Content Referent	Possible Life Skills Topics	Notes

Problem Solving
Determining Reasonable Answers

| UNDERSTAND |
| ANALYZE DATA |
| PLAN |
| ESTIMATE |
| SOLVE |
| EXAMINE |

LEARN ABOUT IT

An important part of evaluating your thinking and work when you solve problems is checking your work. The chart shows some ways to do this.

Examples Do not solve the problem.

Decide if the answer given is reasonable. If it is not reasonable, explain why.

Problem: Jon is 13 years old and weighs 108 pounds. According to the chart, how many calories does he need to consume for each pound of body weight?

Answer: Jon needs to consume 250 calories for each pound.

Check Your Work
- Is the answer reasonable?
- Is the arithmetic correct?
- Did you use the strategies correctly?

Daily Calories			
Boys		**Girls**	
Age	**Calories**	**Age**	**Calories**
1–14	2700	11–14	2200
15–18	2800	15–18	2100

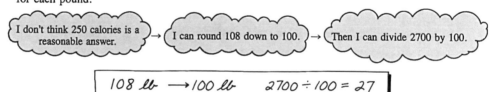

I don't think 250 calories is a reasonable answer. → I can round 108 down to 100. → Then I can divide 2700 by 100.

$$108 \text{ lb} \longrightarrow 100 \text{ lb} \qquad 2700 \div 100 = 27$$

But the correct answer must be less than 27 since I rounded down.

250 calories per pound is not a reasonable answer.

TRY IT OUT

Do not solve the problem. Decide if the answer given is reasonable. If it is not reasonable, explain why.

1. Valerie is 12 years old. For breakfast and lunch she ate a total of 1350 calories. How many calories should she eat for dinner?

   Answer: Valerie should eat 950 calories.

2. A glass of milk has 140 calories. Juan drank 6 glasses of milk. How many calories did the milk have?

   Answer: The milk had 940 calories.

Life Skills Infusion Planning Guide

Note: This planning guide is recommended for use when identifying content in existing curricular materials that can be linked to life skills topics.

Subject Area _____ **Material** _____

Content Referent	Possible Life Skills Topics	Notes

Appendix E
Addresses of Publishers Cited in Examples

Addison-Wesley Longman
2725 Sand Hills Road
Menlo Park, CA 94025

Glencoe McGraw Hill
P.O. Box 9609
Mission Hills, CA 91346

Holt, Rinehart and Winston
6277 Sea Harbor Drive
Orlando, FL 32887

Houghton Mifflin
1560 Sherman Avenue
Evanston, IL 60201

Prentice-Hall, Inc.
Simon & Schuster Education Group
1 Lake Street
Upper Saddle River, NJ 07458

PRO-ED, Inc.
8700 Shoal Creek Boulevard
Austin, Texas 78757

Silver Burdett Ginn
Simon & Schuster Education Group
299 Jefferson Road
Parsippany, NJ 07054

Steck-Vaughn
4515 Seton Center Parkway #300
Austin, Texas 78759

References

Armstrong, D. G. (1990). *Developing and documenting the curriculum*. Boston: Allyn & Bacon.

Brolin, D. E. (1997). *Life centered career education: A competency-based approach* (5th ed.). Reston, VA: The Council for Exceptional Children.

Clark, G. M., & Patton, J. R. (1997). *Transition Planning Inventory*. Austin, TX: PRO-ED.

Clark, G. M., Field, S., Patton, J. R., Brolin, D. E., & Sitlington, P. L. (1994). Life skills instruction: A necessary component for all students with disabilities. A position statement of the Division on Career Development and Transition. *Career Development for Exceptional Individuals, 17*, 125–134.

Cronin, M. E. (1996). Life skills curricula for students with learning disabilities: A review of the literature. *Journal of Learning Disabilities, 29*, 53–68.

Cronin, M. E., & Patton, J. R. (1993). *Life skills instruction for all students with special needs: A practical guide for integrating real-life content into the curriculum*. Austin, TX: PRO-ED.

Dever, R. B. (1988). *Community living skills: A taxonomy*. Washington, DC: American Association on Mental Retardation.

Goals 2000: Educate America Act of 1994, 20 U.S.C. 5801 *et seq.*

Hawaii Transition Project. (1987). Honolulu: University of Hawaii, Department of Special Education.

Helmke, L. M., Havekost, D. M., Patton, J. R., & Polloway, E. A. (1994). Life skills programming: Development of a high school science course. *Teaching Exceptional Children, 26*(2), 49–53.

Hoover, J. J., & Patton, J. R. (1997). *Curriculum adaptations for students with learning and behavior problems: Principles and practices* (2nd ed.). Austin, TX: PRO-ED.

Knowles, M. (1990). *The adult learner: The neglected species* (4th ed.). Houston: Gulf.

Kolstoe, O. P., & Frey, R. M. (1965). *A high school work study program for mentally subnormal students*. Carbondale: Southern Illinois University Press.

National Center on Educational Outcomes. (1993). *Education outcomes and indicators for individuals at the post-school level*. Minneapolis: University of Minnesota.

Rossman, M. (1983). The cheese: An essay on method in science teaching. *Phi Delta Kappan, 64*, 632–634.

School to Work Opportunities Act of 1994, 20 U.S.C. 6101 *et seq.*

Secretary's Commission on Achieving Necessary Skills, U.S. Department of Labor. (1991). *What work requires of schools: A SCANS report for America 2000*. Washington, DC: U.S. Government Printing Office.

Sitlington, P. L. (1996). Transition to living: The neglected components of transition programming for individuals with learning disabilities. *Journal of Learning Disabilities, 29*, 31–39, 52.

Smith, M. A., & Schloss, P. J. (1988). Teaching to transition. In P. J. Schloss, C. A. Hughes, & M. A. Smith (Eds.), *Community integration for persons with mental retardation* (pp. 1–16). Austin, TX: PRO-ED.

About the Authors

James R. Patton is currently the Executive Editor at PRO-ED and an Adjunct Associate Professor at the University of Texas at Austin. He has taught students with special needs at the elementary, secondary, and postsecondary levels in Charlottesville, Virginia, Honolulu, Hawaii, and Austin, Texas. He received a BS in preprofessional studies from the University of Notre Dame and completed his graduate work at the University of Virginia. Dr. Patton's primary areas of professional activity are life skills instruction, transition assessment and planning, lifelong learning, adults with learning disabilities, and accommodating students with special needs in inclusive settings.

Mary E. Cronin is Professor of Special Education and Habilitative Services at the University of New Orleans. She has had experiences in teaching students with special needs at the preschool, elementary, and secondary levels. Her research interests include curriculum development, life skills instruction and materials development, behavior management, transition planning, and instructional needs in inclusive settings. Her current interests include teacher training, life skills program development, and transition issues at each educational level. Mary received her BA from Avila College in Kansas City, Missouri; her MEd from the University of Kansas; and her PhD from the University of Texas at Austin.

Susan J. Wood is a doctoral fellow at the University of New Orleans. Her experience includes teaching students with special needs at the middle and high school levels. Her research interests include life skills, transition issues, applied behavior analysis, and self-management techniques. Currently, she is developing a self-monitoring program for at-risk middle school students. Susan earned a BS in elementary education, a BA in Psychology, and an MEd in special education from Boston University. She has an MEd in educational administration and a PhD in special education from the University of New Orleans.

NOTES

NOTES

NOTES